PIGEON SHOOTING

PIGEON SHOOTING

A Complete Guide

JON HUTCHEON

THE CROWOOD PRESS

First published in 2009 by
The Crowood Press Ltd
Ramsbury, Marlborough
Wiltshire SN8 2HR

www.crowood.com

British Library Cataloguing-in-Publication Data
A catalogue record for this book is available from the British
Library.

ISBN 978 1 84797 123 4

Disclaimer
The author and the publisher do not accept any responsibility in
any manner whatsoever for any error or omission, or any loss,
damage, injury, adverse outcome, or liability of any kind incurred
as a result of the use of any of the information contained in this
book, or reliance upon it. If in doubt about any aspect of pigeon
shooting readers are advised to seek professional advice.

Line illustrations by Keith Field

Photographs by the author unless otherwise stated

Typeset by Magenta Publishing Ltd (www.magentapublishing.com)

Printed and bound in Singapore by Craft Print International

CONTENTS

Dedication   6

Introduction   7

1   The Quarry   11

2   Equipment   28

3   Guns and Safety   55

4   Shooting Over Decoys   83

5   Roost Shooting   99

6   Barn Shooting   107

7   Rough Shooting   111

8   The Bag   117

Glossary   121

Useful Information   123

Index   124

DEDICATION

As always, I dedicate this book first and foremost to my long-suffering and much-loved wife and children. Without their continuous support and positive outlook the book would have never have been written. I would also like to thank those landowners who have allowed me access to their property to pursue my sport. Additionally, my good friend Graham cannot be forgotten, as his knowledge and advice have provided much insight and guidance over the past decade. I must also thank Chris for giving me my early opportunities at the 'Woodies'. Finally, I would like to thank BDR Trading of Worthing, West Sussex for their help with clothing and photos.

INTRODUCTION

I will confess to thinking long and hard before compiling this book. There has been much written about pigeon shooting, so I needed to be sure that I could write a truly worthy manuscript before putting the proverbial pen to paper. Those of you who are familiar with my previous publications will be well aware that they centre around the pursuit of rabbits with dogs, ferrets, nets and traps. I have written extensively on these subjects and they are indeed areas for which I have an infinite passion. That said, I am also an extremely keen shot.

Over the years, I have been lucky enough to shoot pretty much all of the quarry species found within the UK, the only exception being grouse. I have shot driven pheasants and partridge and have had the pleasure of inland and foreshore wild fowling. This has allowed me to bag Canada geese, snipe and woodcock as well as 'long tails' and those fast and agile red legs. Then, of course, there have been the various mammalian species that I have bagged. I do truly enjoy shooting, particularly with air rifles and shotguns. I have an unrivalled passion for the .410. This often overlooked calibre of shotgun is in fact my first choice of weapon when in the field. It suits my needs perfectly, as it is light to carry and relatively quiet.

Throughout all of my shooting experiences the one avian quarry species that I have continually pursued is the pigeon, in both its feral and wood forms. Therefore, when reflecting on my own experiences in the field, I drew the conclusion that I am indeed more than qualified to pen a manuscript based on the subject of pigeon shooting. In addition to this, my shooting partner is affectionately known as the 'pigeon man'. As a result, with his help and added experience (he is twenty years my senior), everything has fallen nicely into place.

Something that I have been very conscious of are the changes in the sport of pigeon shooting that have occurred over the past decade or more. When I first shot pigeons it was still known to a degree as the 'poor man's sport', the pastime of your 'average Joe'. It was the shooting that the person who could not afford to shoot driven game would have to settle for. Game shooters often overlooked pigeon shooting and disregarded its value as a form of field sport. I am not talking here about the fifties and sixties. I am only in my thirties so I am, in fact, talking about the late eighties and early nineties.

Ironically, pigeon shooting was once very much the sport of the gentry. This, however, was not pigeon shooting as we now know it. In the nineteenth century, before such things as conservation had even been considered by most shooting men, pigeon shooting was a very popular pastime. Live pigeons would have been caged and released for the sporting gentleman to shoot at with his muzzle loader. This was considered to be a way to practise your shooting, and also a form of entertainment on which wagers would often be placed. I suppose that, these days, the equivalent is clay pigeon shooting, which sees the live bird replaced with clay disks. It is easy for us to criticize our ancestors for taking part in this sort of shooting with live game. However, we should perhaps remember that this was practiced in a time when game was plentiful and species of animals becoming extinct as a result of over-hunting was still not something that anyone knew about. After all, the world was very much still being explored and discovered.

In the last decade or so, the pastime of pigeon shooting has seen some dramatic changes. Incidentally, I will refer to it as a sport but must state that it is actually a form of pest control. In fact, for reasons we shall look at in a later chapter, it is essential to shoot pigeons for pest control purposes and not just for the thrill of it. With regards to the significant changes to pigeon shooting, it is no longer the poor man's pastime and has become, in some cases, a sought-after activity for the majority of shooters. Many game shots will now shoot pigeons over the summer months to ensure that they keep their hand in. Of course, clay pigeon shooting does allow for this to a degree but a rather important secret now seems to be out of the bag; many people have begun to recognize just what a diverse sporting experience pigeon shooting can offer.

The thing with pigeon shooting is that the birds will never fly in exactly the same way. Of course, they will come from the same direction or angle, but no two birds will be identical. The wind will alter their speed and approach, and this is what makes the pastime so appealing to me and, I am sure, to many others. This, combined with the number of pigeons within the UK, is what I feel has made the pastime so popular. As well as the residential birds that live here, there are also migratory flocks, and the indications are that numbers are on the increase, not

the decrease. This, therefore, gives plenty of opportunity for the shooting person to partake in the pastime.

Pigeon shooting has become so popular that there are even syndicates and pigeon clubs. These clubs allow members to shoot over vast expanses of ground for a small yearly fee. In addition to this, there are numerous pigeon guides who provide the chance to shoot for those who, otherwise, would not have ground to shoot over. These guides secure vast areas of land and they specialize in taking people shooting and ensuring that the birds fly in the right direction, or more to the point that the shooter is in the right place. When I was in my teens, pigeon shooting on an estate was often a perk for the regular beaters and farm workers. These days many estates save the sport for the paying guns to enjoy.

Although all of the above looks like a good thing for field sports, and indeed the countryside, as it helps to create revenue and control a listed pest species, I have mixed thoughts on just how good it is in reality. The more 'professional' the sport becomes, the harder I feel it will be made for the lone shooter or pot hunter to find shooting. In addition to this, it is all very well getting someone to find the pigeons for you – and in some cases to set up all of the kit – allowing you simply to sit back and pull the trigger, but what about the field craft? When I was first taken pigeon shooting I was taught how to find the birds, how to recognize where they were feeding and, just as importantly, where they would roost. I learnt how to judge the range of a shot and how to set up a decoy pattern correctly. I learnt how essential observation and field craft was and that, in order to enjoy any sport, you had to invest time into these things. My concern is that there is a chance that the twenty-first century shooter could be at risk of losing these skills. Again, let us not forget that the shooting of pigeons is predominantly a pest control exercise. We live in a time when field sports of all sorts are under constant scrutiny and it is imperative that those who participate in them understand fully why they are shooting a species. Therefore, it is this aspect of the pastime to which I want to dedicate time and effort within the pages of this book.

I will endeavour to show you the skills needed to find and locate your quarry, and will then explain what you have to do in order to shoot it with any degree of success. I am not just talking about shooting over crops with decoys, but also about roost shooting and even feral pigeon shooting around buildings. Most importantly, I want to ensure that the quarry is respected and, above all, used. Despite the fact that pigeon is a pest species, it is a truly delicious meat, and all the more so because it is as free range as can be. One thing that truly saddens me is seeing produce that is shot being wasted. To my mind, if you are going to shoot or kill any species you should, whenever possible, use it. I accept that there are a few species that cannot be eaten, but pigeons are certainly not one of them. I shall, therefore, also dedicate some time to explaining how to prepare and enjoy the fruits of your labour.

Of course, while doing this I will try not to overlook the modern aspect of the pastime. These days there are far more options than a branch clad hide in the side of a hedge and a few plastic decoys. The modern pigeon shooter has a range of weird and wonderful contraptions at their disposal. There are decoys that flap and whirl, there are springing devices and even nodding plastic pecking decoys. Then

there is a huge range of camouflage products, all of which claim to make you so invisible that nothing will see you. These take the shape of hides as well as clothing, and the market is truly inundated with different pieces of kit.

If I was naïve, I could suggest that many of these items are perhaps a result of the rather consumer-controlled market that we live in. I could suggest that it is possible to shoot just as well without some of these modern contraptions, and that perhaps not all of these modern wonders are needed to have success. Of course, it would be negligent of me to suggest this, as surely much of this equipment must be necessary – at least you would think so when you look through some shooting magazines. What I will do, however, is try to demonstrate how you can combine many of these modern pieces of kit with home-made items. As someone whose pockets are continually empty, this is an imperative aspect of my shooting. I simply do not have the cash to splash on the latest gadgets and gizmos. Therefore, a little field sports DIY is an essential part of my sport.

I have been involved with all sorts of field sports for the majority of my life. I have an inbred affinity that I simply cannot override, and to me field sports are not a hobby, they are a passion and way of life.

I grew up in the suburban surroundings of Sussex and, in truth, I cannot really say where the 'hunting gene' in me comes from. Perhaps it comes from my father's Scottish ancestors who, I believe, enjoyed a rural life style. Another aspect comes, without doubt, from the input I received as a child when my parents would regularly visit my grandparents in rural Devon. It was on a family friend's farm that I was first introduced to the joys of the great outdoors and, by the age of ten, it was clear that shooting and rural pastimes were with me for good. It was around this time that I began to beat on a local pheasant shoot and eventually to help the keeper once the season had finished. This, ironically, was all thanks to another family friend who kindly introduced me to pigeon shooting with my bolt action Webley .410.

By the age of fifteen I had decided that the educational route was not particularly for me. I spent all of my school days wishing to be out in the fresh air, and leaving school was a welcome occasion. I then commenced work as an assistant gamekeeper on a local shoot but for various reasons, and much to the surprise of everyone (especially me), I soon left the job. I spent the next few years exploring various options but never lost interest in the countryside and gamekeeping. Now, fifteen years on, I am more involved with rural pursuits than ever. Over the last decade, as well as holding down my 'normal job', I have continued to work within gamekeeping. I have also worked as a woodsman and have undertaken various farm work. My interest in field sports has continued to expand and I have a great love for the link of conservation with field sports. I also control vermin – mainly rabbits – over several thousand acres in the South of England.

The time I do not spend out shooting, netting or working my lurcher and ferrets is spent tending to my horses and livestock. Any spare time is dedicated to trying to promote field sports, especially to the younger generations and to those who have no knowledge of the subjects. The countryside is not just somewhere I like to be, it is in my soul and without it I feel I would struggle to survive. My hope through my writing is to pass on what knowledge I have to others, including my own children. I aim to do all of this in as down-to-earth a manner as I possibly can. I am not an expert, I am simply someone who has been lucky and has the opportunity to share his knowledge with others.

Finally, a note regarding measurements. When shooting distances are referred to in the book, usually to indicate the distances at which your shot will be most effective with a particular gun, I have used yards without a metric conversion. As 1yd is roughly equal to 0.9m, it seems unnecessary to clutter the text with conversions.

CHAPTER 1

THE QUARRY

THE WOOD PIGEON

The wood pigeon (*Columba palumbus*) is an easily recognizable bird to the field sportsman, pest controller and bird watcher. Its soothing 'coo, coo' is often to be heard gently drifting across the countryside. The bird is also extremely easy to identify with its grey plumage, white neck ring and white wing bar. The tail and flight feathers are black and the legs pink. Finally, the beak is yellow with a pink base.

The wood pigeon is a resident species that lives in the UK throughout the year. It is estimated that there are between 2 and 2.5 million breeding pairs within Britain and between 9 and 12 million pairs across Europe. Around half of this population is found in Britain, France and Germany. The resident pigeons living in Britain are added to throughout the winter by migrating birds travelling across Europe. Many of these birds will stop to feed, and without doubt some will remain and become resident within the UK.

The birds breed between April and September, although with the constant climate changes that are going on around us I would not be surprised if this changes in the not too distant future. More regularly, I am seeing the seasons blend into

A flock of feral pigeons coming in to roost and feed on the farmer's corn stored in the barn. (© Bruce Potts of Sylvan Films)

The wood pigeon.

one. Rabbits that used to be pursued in every month with an 'R', as this was when they did not breed, now have young all year through. Foxes tend to have cubs earlier than ever, and I even saw a pheasant hen with chicks in October. I am sure that the migratory habits of many avian species will change, and I have no doubt that this will include the wood pigeon.

On average there will be three or four clutches of two eggs. Incubation lasts for seventeen days and the young fledge for twenty-nine to thirty-five days. Pigeon nests look rather messy and consist of a platform of twigs and leaves that do not hold the tidy shaping of many of our avian species. Both sexes of birds build the nests and, although they do travel in flocks during the breeding season, it is common to see pairs within flocks or alone.

Wood pigeons, as the name suggests, reside in wooded areas and move out to feed, normally at first light. They will return to feed at dusk. However, during the summer months you will often find, especially on those arduously hot days, that the birds will feed with more conviction in the late afternoon and evening. The type of food they are eating varies according to the time of year. All arable crops are popular with wood pigeons. Particular attention should be paid to crops that are sown in the winter, especially when other food is sparse. This includes such things as rape and sugar beat or maize. As spring becomes more noticeable, the birds will turn their attention to drilled cereals and fresh crops of peas or beans. Clover is another popular food source at this time, and grass drillings should also be monitored for signs of damage.

When cereal and arable crops are at their best in the summer, the birds have a wide choice of foods available. Flat spots in wheat and barley will swiftly be targeted, as will standing crops of beans and peas. Set-aside and freshly sewn game cover will also prove an irresistible lure for most hungry wood pigeons. Late summer and early autumn will see the birds hitting the stubbles and clearing any left over grains before they move onto any drillings for winter crops. In the winter months they will clean up the acorns around any relevant wooded areas and this, combined with the many berries available, will give most farmers a slight break in the crop damage. The birds will also feed over any stubble fields left for the winter and, of course, on any accessible root crops, including potatoes.

As you will see from the brief insight given above, the wood pigeon, given its numbers and feeding habits, presents a real issue for any arable farmer. It should, therefore, be no surprise that the bird is managed for pest control purposes given the potential damage that a flock of birds can do to a field of arable/cereal. Of course, the wood pigeon is not the only bird to feed on arable crops, and consideration is given to which birds can and cannot be controlled by culling. It is important that if you intend to shoot wood pigeons, or any other birds, you fully understand this.

THE WILDLIFE AND COUNTRYSIDE ACT, 1981

Before we expand in any more detail with regards to finding pigeons and locating them with an intention to control their numbers, let us first look at the Wildlife and Countryside Act and, in particular, the 'general licence' held within it. The Wildlife and Countryside Act was set up to protect wild animals and plants from any unnecessary suffering and/or damage. Within the Act there is a range of 'general licences' that set out which species can or cannot be culled, and when the culling can and cannot take place. With regards to the wood pigeon, we need to concern ourselves with the 'licence to kill or take certain birds to prevent serious damage or disease'.

It is easy to think that you can simply grab a gun and go and shoot a pigeon at your leisure. To a degree this may be the case, but the 'general licence' sets out some important guidance notes that any sensible person should be aware of before pursuing their chosen quarry. Firstly, and

Mixed pigeon country that includes a vineyard, woodland and stubble in the background.

Arable crops towards the tail end of the summer.

foremost under the terms of the licence that is governed by an organization called Natural England, the species within it can only be controlled in a bid to prevent the spread of disease or to prevent serious damage to livestock, foodstuffs for livestock, crops, vegetables, fruit, growing timber, fisheries or inland waters. Secondly, you must be satisfied that non-lethal methods of resolving any issues such as crop damage are ineffective and impracticable before you go about killing any species covered by the licence.

In simple terms, you are quite entitled to shoot pigeons if you can justify that the birds are causing crop damage and that they cannot be stopped from doing so. In most cases trying to stop pigeons from feeding on a crop is an impossible task. Perhaps bangers may have been tried or scarecrows or flags put up to deter the birds. Usually all this does is move them to another field or further down the crop they are on. They will also adjust to any noise, flag or deterrent in a pretty short space of time so it is, I feel, fair to say that you will always have grounds under the 'general licence' to shoot pigeons – at least while the licence is in its current form and not amended.

There are, of course, possible exceptions, and I feel a paragraph or two should be invested in discussing these. Firstly, let us take a situation where pigeons are residing in a large wood that is situated on a farm that has no arable crops. Let us say that you have permission to shoot in this wood and your intention is to pick up the pigeons as they fly in to roost. The question that I would ask is, technically, should you be shooting these birds or not? Are they causing damage to crops on the land? The answer will be no but that does not mean you are acting against the law if you shoot them.

Remember, the licence states: 'The purpose for which this licence is granted are preventing the spread of disease and preventing serious damage to livestock, foodstuffs for livestock, crops, vegetables, fruit, growing timber, fisheries or inland water'. With this in mind you can, therefore, argue that the droppings from the pigeons could spread disease and, in fact, even if foodstuffs are not grown on the farm in question but are next door, you will still have a case for controlling the species. The trees that the birds are roosting in may also be used for timber. The point I am making by including this example is to show that you really do need to be aware of the 'general licence' and its content. In these politically correct times that we live in, shooting is under constant scrutiny and, as a result, it is imperative that those of us who are in engaged in pigeon shooting are fully aware of what we are doing and why we are doing it.

The Wildlife and Countryside Act is also in place to protect wildlife from unnecessary suffering and this is again something that the pigeon shooter should be aware

Taking a shot from a hide.

Pigeon droppings in the floor of a barn. This is from no more than a half a dozen birds.

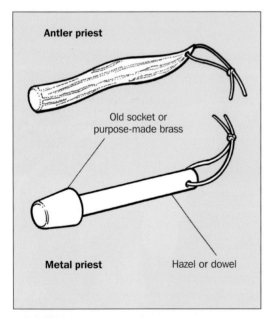

Two diagrams of priests. The first is an antler priest that is naturally weighted and measures no more than 9in long. The second is weighted with a brass end or with an old socket fitted onto a hazel or dowel handle.

of. Birds should be dispatched quickly and swiftly, and the dispatching should be done in a clean and efficient manner. I would advise the use of a priest to knock the bird on the back of the head, a humane game dispatch tool (this resembles a pair of pliers and breaks the neck) or a method of breaking the neck via twisting it quickly. You must never leave a wounded bird and all birds should be retrieved for dispatch if not dead.

There are many more areas of the Act that could be explored, but I feel for the purpose of this book we need only cover one more essential point. This point is that the 'general licence' permits authorized persons to carry out the activities that it sets out. Again this is also a crucial factor, as if you are not authorized by the relevant party you will be in breach of the Act and licence. This is something we shall touch on when we explore the law relating to shooting.

At the time of writing the following species can be culled under general licence. The licence is reviewed yearly and those species that are listed can, and do, change from time to time.

- Greater Canada goose
- Crow
- Collared dove
- Greater and lesser black-backed gull
- Herring gull
- Jackdaw
- Jay
- Magpie
- Feral pigeon and wood pigeon
- Rook

It is not necessary to explain the details of all of these species, but some of them will without doubt be 'fair game' when you are pigeon shooting. Therefore, it is important

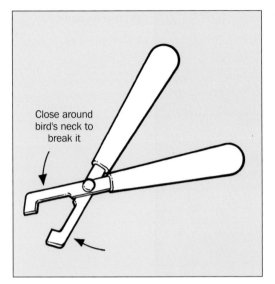

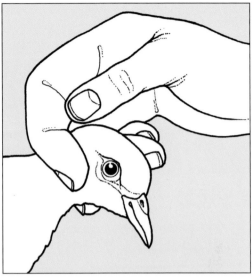

A diagram of a humane game dispatching tool, they operate like pliers and are used around the bird's neck to break it.

To kill a pigeon hold the head between your fourth finger and middle finger. Pull the head down and then slightly upwards to break the bird's neck.

A feral pigeon nest in a barn roof.

A crow on stubble.

A magpie with its distinctive black and white colour. The feathers are actually green and blue on closer inspection.

that you can identify these birds when in the field. With regards to corvids such as rooks, crows and magpies, identity is relatively easy. Crows and rooks are black in colour and crows have black beaks while rooks have grey beaks. Magpies are smaller than crows and rooks and have the tell-tale black markings. In some areas of the UK crows also come in a hooded variety. Hooded crows are also white and black but much larger than magpies. The jackdaw is also a member of the corvid family and is also jet black with a black beak, but is half the size of a crow or rook. The only odd one out within corvids is the jay. This bird is a bright brown/red colour with white, black and blue markings covering its face and wings.

Feral pigeons are the sort that you will often see milling around town squares and sat in multi-storey car parks. They are fair game and will often travel in large and small flocks. Colours will vary and care should be taken not to confuse feral pigeons with racing pigeons. Racing pigeons are normally distinguished by the way that they fly and focus on doing this and this alone. You should never shoot racing pigeons, and care should be taken to be sure that you identify a feral from a racing pigeon before shooting.

Collared doves are much smaller than feral and wood pigeons, they are sandy in colour and have a black neck band. They tend to travel in small flocks and pairs. These birds will often be found around farm buildings but will drop into decoys when shooting wood pigeons. Care should

A feral pigeon sitting on a barn roof at dusk. It can be very hard to distinguish between this and a racing pigeon at such a distance.

A racing pigeon with its ring clearly visible.

19

also be taken not to shoot stock doves that often mix with flocks of wood pigeons. They are distinguishable as they are smaller and grey all over. They have black wing bars and a faster wing beat than the wood pigeon. Rock doves are also protected and are very similar in appearance to stock doves, they have a noticeable white under rump.

FINDING THE BIRDS

You will only be successful when shooting pigeons if you can learn to locate the pigeons and where they are feeding. This again may sound like common sense but as with all field sports there is a little more to it than just seeing some birds eating on a field. You also need to work out which way the birds will depart the area and indeed fly into it. It is also helpful to have an idea of the roosting area and the times that the birds seem to be feeding. There will be numerous factors that will influence this and, consequently, your success in shooting any birds in reasonable numbers.

Do not be fooled by stories of a hundred birds being shot per day, every day with ease. This does happen but not just like that. It is the result of planning, reconnaissance and often many hours spent in the field. The first thing to consider is the time of year. In the winter months, as we have already discussed, the birds move as a flock. Thousands of pigeons may descend on a field and the sight can be quite inspiring. The immediate reaction is to rush out and set up where the birds are feeding and to begin banging away. The problem is that if you do this there is every chance that the whole flock will disappear with

A wood pigeon feeding on the ground.

The collared dove. (© Bruce Potts of Sylvan Films)

the first crack of a shotgun and move onto another feeding ground.

The first thing you should do is assess what other foodstuffs are growing in the vicinity. If every field is covered with rape, for example, and this is what the birds are feeding on, they will simply move from one field to another. With this situation there are two appropriate actions. Firstly, you need to try to prevent the birds from feeding on every field. Your aim is to try and funnel them to one area so they can be culled effectively. This could be done by arranging for bangers to be set out in areas to discourage feeding or deterrents such as flapping bags to be set up. These methods will work, but the birds will also get used to them. Therefore, the art is to set the deterrent up perhaps for two or three days and then to cull the birds before they become wise to the situation.

The second option is to go out with other guns and to set up in different locations. By doing this the birds will be kept moving from field to field and the risk of them vanishing is kept to a minimum. I must, however, add that both of these methods are best suited to larger sized farms. Of course, the danger on a small area is that the birds simply fly over the border and feed next door.

The ideal situation with a flock of birds is to have them feeding on one food source that they seem drawn to and simply do not want to leave. The problem is that with modern agriculture many

21

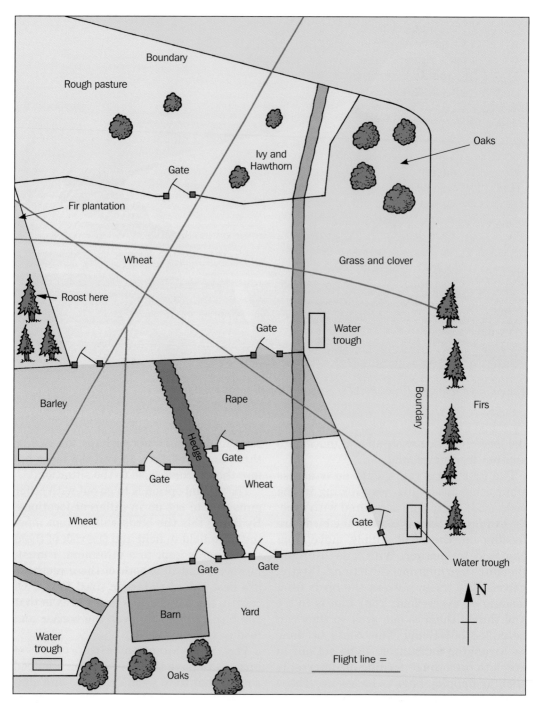

A rough map of some shooting ground with all the important features highlighted.

farms will just blanket plough the same crop. This gives vast feeding areas that can be difficult to cover. A more preferable scenario would be for the crops to be staggered with different crops growing at different stages. If you are lucky enough to have a farm to shoot over that grows crops at different stages throughout the year it will make controlling the pigeons a great deal easier.

Having considered the above, I would urge you to take a systematic plan of attack before you begin shooting. Firstly, take a good hard look at the ground you are shooting over. Take a map and mark on the wooded areas and any other prominent pigeon locations. Walk the farm and look for signs of pigeon droppings and feathers. This will enable you to gain a knowledge of where the birds are roosting. Pigeons will not simply settle for any old area. They like to tuck up in the areas of woodland that will provide them with some warmth and shelter. Fir trees are always popular, as are areas that contain ivy. The birds will get right inside the ivy and have the additional advantage of the berries as a food source.

If you have great expanses of woodland, finding the roosts can be a rather tricky task. While walking through them you may well spot the odd feather followed by another and another. Then you may see droppings and as you look up you will see yet more droppings on the trees and feathers on the branches. The problem is that sometimes the harder you look the harder it is to find the right area. In this case I would suggest stepping back and viewing the area from a distance. If you do this at first light and dusk you will see the birds flying to and fro. This will indicate where they are heading for and you can then review the area at a closer level.

Smaller blocks of woodland are a much easier affair to deal with. It stands to reason that if the birds have only a limited area in which to roost, then they have to go for what is open to them and cannot be too fussy. I relish those wonderful farms that hold the odd half acre of firs here and the spinny of oaks there. On these sorts of areas you can almost guess where the birds will roost before looking. Roosts will not just be limited to wooded areas. In the summer months the birds will often choose the cool of a large dead old tree stood alone along a fence line. Likewise a roundel of broad oaks will offer a welcome shelter from the midday sun. Telegraph poles and wires will also be a popular choice for a pigeon to take a rest, especially on a hot day. As well as identifying the roosts, I would also advise noting down where any water troughs are located. Also note down the location of ponds and even streams or rivers. Pigeons need to drink and it is amazing just how often a flight line that goes from a feeding ground to roost cuts across a water trough or dew pond.

Mapping your ground in this manner not only allows you to have a better understanding of where the birds are feeding and living, it also provides you with the chance to identify any footpaths, bridleways and hazards. You can learn which areas will not be practical to shoot over and, just as importantly, find those little nooks and crannies that will give you a natural hiding place. When looking for hazards do not only consider those at ground level. You should also watch for phone and power lines, which should be avoided for obvious reasons.

Once you have a good understanding of the habits of the quarry the next step is to look to the skies again. I have touched

These downlands have flight lines that follow the contours, and plenty of roosting places.

briefly on the subject of flight lines, and this is something that I feel we should now look at in more detail. A flight line is the route that birds will use in order to travel to and from a set area. This line generally gives them the best view of where they are coming from and going to. The birds will follow the same line and, thus, if you get the route of the flight line it gives an ideal location from which you will be able to target the birds. There will be some lines that are continuously used. These will often follow the contours of the land and in some cases will be used year in, year out. There will also be lines that become established when the birds need to feed on a crop that has been sewn. These will change as the crops change.

Again, it is tempting to think that shooting pigeons is an easy process, alas this is not the case. Often there will be more than one flight line going to and from a feeding area or roosting site. The lines will alter depending on the wind and the direction that the birds need to take in order to reach their destination. All too often a feeding area will have three or four lines coming to it from different angles. You could set up directly under one line and you will be able to let some shots off. On the other hand, if you can, the best situation is to set up in a location between the lines. If the birds are being decoyed, they will then pull in towards you not from one line of flight but from all of them. This is how you go about bagging large quantities of pigeons, especially in the summer months when the birds are paired and not flocked.

Before we move on to look at the equipment needed for pigeon shooting, there are a few other important factors to discuss with regards to the quarry. The first thing to consider is timing, especially when decoying. In the winter months the birds will often feed throughout the day; from dawn until dusk. You could end up shooting continuously and enjoy some great sport. The thing to remember is that we are talking about the winter. I know that it is not as cold as it used to be so, if the birds do come in fast, you will be kept warm as you move, mount and shoot. However, considering the comfort and angle of sitting in a net-covered hide with a stiff wind blowing around you all day long, if the birds do not play ball you will soon end up cold and dispirited. My suggestion is therefore a simple one. In the winter months set up as the birds come from roost so that you can shoot for the morning and pack up at midday. This will allow you a chance to warm up for a couple of hours. You can then continue to shoot for that last hour or so before roosting time, or you could simply pack up the decoys and enjoy an hour's roost shooting to vary your sport.

In the summer months the temptation can again be to shoot all day. From my experience this can pay off but, more often than not, you will find again that shooting in the morning or afternoon can be the best option. If the weather is particularly warm the birds will often feed from dawn through to midday. At this point, when the heat is at its worst, they will often retreat to the shelter of some big shady trees. You may then experience three or four hours of barely a single movement from a pigeon, especially during the height of summer. My advice for summer pigeon shooting is to either start with the birds at dawn and to shoot until they ease up, normally at lunch time as stated. Alternatively, and this is my favoured approach, start later in the afternoon and shoot until the birds

go to roost. The difference with this as opposed to winter shooting is that it will be late into the evening. The added advantage of shooting in the latter part of the day is that the birds that have refrained from feeding in the morning will, without fail, feed before roosting.

In reality, the only time I would consider shooting from early morning until late in the day is during the spring. Personally, I find that as much as I enjoy pigeon shooting, banging away with a gun for anything more than four or so hours becomes a little tedious. I prefer good steady shooting over a sensible time scale. This allows me to take plenty of birds from a pest control perspective and also gives me some varied sport. For me, shooting is a way to relax as much as anything else. It is surprising just how much concentration you need when pigeon shooting, and if you spend too long out you can become disillusioned with the process. This is especially true if the birds, as described, stop flying in the summer heat. It is all too easy to spend two or three hours becoming frustrated in the confines of a hide. By the time the pigeons start to fly in again you are often in the wrong mindset. Your shooting becomes poor and a good day becomes somewhat marred.

OTHER QUARRY

Although this book is aimed at pigeon shooting there are some other avian species that I feel it would be wrong not to mention. There are three types of birds that, in the majority of cases, the pigeon shooter will generally also have the opportunity to shoot. These are rooks, crows and magpies. All of these birds are from the corvid family and, like the pigeon, they can be shot all year round. Corvids

A plastic rook or crow decoy.

are a totally different kettle of fish to shoot compared to pigeons. Pigeons will generally decoy in provided you have concealed yourself with relative success, corvids on the other hand will not decoy in unless you are completely invisible.

In truth, a separate book could be written on the subject of controlling corvids, and my aim is certainly not to give chapter and verse details on specifically decoying or hunting this family. What I would like to do in brief is explain how and why you may need to shoot these species when pigeon shooting. Firstly, the rook as a species is both a blessing and a curse to farmers. It will assist a great deal of the time as it eats slugs and other parasites that will target arable crops. The problem is that rooks will also eat the crops themselves, especially cereal-based crops. As a result, it can pay to leave rooks alone for much of the year. The method I find works the best is to thin out the young rooks in May and then target the adults in the summer when the wheat and barley has those

golden ears swaying in the wind. Rooks, like pigeons, need access to a source of water, so setting up to shoot both pigeons and rooks by a trough or pond can pay dividends. Another great place to set up for rooks is by dung heaps. They head to these areas to feed on the beatles and worms that fill them. If you have a field that is sewn with a crop targeted by pigeons and rooks alike, and there is a dung heap in the corner of the field or between some flight lines, this could prove an excellent spot at which to set up.

Rooks can and will respond to decoys. I always find that it pays when setting up a pattern of pigeon decoys to set a couple of rook or crow decoys out on the fringes of the pattern. This not only pulls in the rooks but also helps to build confidence in any pigeons. The woodies seem to know the qualities of corvids and the sight of one, albeit a plastic one on the edge of a decoy pattern, will make a noticeable difference to how the birds pull in. I must stress, however, that I am not talking about more than one or two corvid decoys. If you put too many out with pigeon decoys they will often have the reverse affect.

Crows and magpies will respond to decoys but tend to be much harder to pull in than rooks. Like pigeons, rooks tend to flock, whereas magpies tend to group and crows tend to pair. Magpies will show little interest in decoys, and if you do get a shot at one it is generally more by luck than anything else. Crows will show an interest in decoys but are extremely cautious and will often circle high on the thermals before coming within range. When they do come downwards, the slightest movement will send them spiralling away. Unlike the rook, most farmers will be more than happy for crows and magpies to be shot all the year through. The birds are notorious egg thieves and can play havoc on the smaller species of 'garden birds' and also game birds, especially during the spring and early summer. There are, of course, other species of corvid that can be shot including the jay and the jackdaw. It is, however, the aforementioned three that I feel you will be most likely to encounter. Nevertheless, I would stress that you should not shoot anything other than pigeons unless the farmer or landowner specifically tells you that you can.

We have concentrated on the wood pigeon to this point so I would like to conclude this chapter with a brief look at the feral pigeon. These birds are of mixed colour and shape and will often feed alongside wood pigeons. Although they will roost in trees, they often prefer to reside on the

Feral pigeons are often found feeding within towns and urban areas.

beams of barns or on the roofs of any farm buildings they can get to. If you shoot on the outskirts of a large town or city you will often find the feral birds coming out of the town to feed on the crops in numbers far outnumbering the wood pigeons. Feral pigeons can be shot legally but it is important to note that you should never shoot or target racing pigeons. You may now be asking how you tell the difference.

The simplest way is to note the difference in habit between the two types of birds. Racing pigeons will be flying in a direct straight flight but will seldom show interest in decoys. They will also seldom roost in buildings and will only set down for a short rest or a drink. Feral pigeons will respond to decoy patterns just like wood pigeons and will follow similar feeding and roosting patterns with regards to times and location.

CHAPTER 2

EQUIPMENT

Now that I have given you an insight into the quarry and how to locate it, I feel the time is right to turn our attention to the type of equipment that you will need in order to have any success in the field. Any prices quoted in this chapter are given to the best of my knowledge at the time of writing, and are intended only to act as a guideline for the reader. The necessary equipment can be broken down into four categories. These are as follows:

- Clothing
- Decoys
- Hides
- Accessories

CLOTHING

Clothing plays a vital part in the majority of sports and pastimes and shooting is no exception to this. Your clothing needs to be comfortable and also suitable for the activity in which you are participating. For the pigeon shooter, I would suggest that your clothing needs to be picked using two main thought processes. The first is comfort, as if your clothing does not fit or hang correctly it will affect your shooting. Secondly, you should consider the colour of your 'outfits'. You do not want anything too bright or noticeable for obvious reasons.

General Fit

Everyone has different ideas as to what sort of fit clothing should have in order to be comfortable; some like their clothes tight and snug, while others prefer them loose and baggy. My guidance with regards to picking the right attire for shooting is to look at the activity you are going to be doing and then ensure that you have the correct clothing from there. On a hot day the last thing you want is to be bogged down in a pair of heavy trousers and a mammoth sized jacket that weighs as much as you do. You would be far better placed with a lightweight shirt or t-shirt and some light cotton trousers.

In the winter, when the wind is biting and the cold sends chills up your legs, wear a heavier form of trousers. A jacket will be a must but do not fall into the trap of wearing several layers under it that make it impossible for you to handle a gun with ease. This may all sound like common sense, but we can all get it wrong from time to time. I always avoid an excessive amount of pockets in my upper garments. Having too many pockets causes two problems. One is that the gun can get snagged when you raise it to shoot. The other is that you fill them with so much rubbish that you can either weigh yourself down or end up not being able to find something in a hurry. I also try to avoid trousers and jackets that are riddled with catches, latches and draw strings. I find that simplicity works best. A couple of buttons and a zip is all that is required and anything more than this can become a hassle and a chore. Again, too many additions means that more things can get snagged up or rattle and clatter about.

I feel that it is also appropriate to mention something with regards to head, toe and finger wear. I would strongly advise that you consider your comfort with regards to socks, gloves and a hat. If you are shooting from a hide, your face and hands will stick out like a sore thumb and it makes sense to cover them. As with coats and jackets though, please do not go out in the summer heat in a pair of thick woolly or leather shooting gloves. Your fingers will sweat and itch and your gun handling will suffer. Get a nice lightweight pair of gloves for summer and something heavier for winter. Likewise, wear sensible head attire for the time of year. A woolly hat or balaclava will be great in December but terrible in July. A lightweight scrim mask or net/mesh head veil will be far more appropriate for the summer months.

Footwear really is important as there is nothing worse than suffering with either cold or sweaty feet. Therefore, opt for the best thing for the time of year. I wear heavy socks in winter with a leather boot that insulates my feet. In the summer a light sock with a canvas and leather desert style boot or a trainer or walking boot is ideal and extremely comfortable.

Camouflage

The obvious choice of attire for many pigeon shooters is camouflaged clothing. I would suggest that this can be broken down into two categories: purpose-designed 'leisure wear' items, and military

Close-up of hat and scrim mask.

surplus items. The leisure wear type of clothing that I refer to is the sort that now comes in nearly every style imaginable and follows the pattern of a tree or wilderness design. This clothing is available from a vast range of suppliers and there really is a huge choice of garments available. The idea of this sort of camouflage is that it mimics the design of the natural area and you seem to disappear when you wear it in the right location.

You only have to flick through the pages of any shooting magazine to see just how popular this sort of camouflage is. It would be wrong of me to try and discredit these items as I do own some myself. My concern, however, is that at times they are so good that I feel it is easy for novices to field sports to assume that all they need is to cover themselves from head to toe in a bush blending outfit and away they go. It can be easy to assume that the clothes will lead to success, and to forget that you will also need field craft to truly understand and learn how to hunt and catch your quarry. I would suggest that, as good as this clothing is, you can still become just as good and catch just as much if you were not wearing it providing you learn the correct way to hunt your quarry, and you do not go out in bright yellow and orange garments.

It seems that, in the twenty-first century, this sort of camouflage has been adopted as the uniform of the field sports participators who enjoy their sport away from the environment of the formal

Non-military camouflage.

driven shooting. With these patterns being sold on everything from lightweight summer coats and t-shirts to heavy winter waterproof jackets, I suppose this is no surprise – and there are a very good range of items available. The cost of this sort of clothing varies depending on the pattern and style, but a pair of trousers can be purchased from £30 upwards and a jacket from £40 upwards, although I must stress it really will depend on the style and make. You can also find lightweight mesh suits that can be worn over your normal clothing. These are great, and cheap for what you get.

Military style camouflage is a different design altogether and is much more basic. The colours tend to come in a blend and generally you will find the basic DPM (green/brown/black) pattern and the desert pattern worn currently in the Gulf. You can also get different patterns from different countries, such as the German 'fleckarm' pattern. Personally I find military camouflage just as effective as the purpose-designed wear previously described. There are also other styles and patterns available, some of which, it must be said, are not that far off from the 'leisure wear' style of design. With military style camouflage you do tend to have a slightly more limited range of design than the purpose-designed camouflage lines. The advantage, however, especially if you are on a budget, is that it can be purchased at a much cheaper price. Military clothing is often sold as surplus stock and is graded depended on its quality. If you are after something for shooting as opposed to fashion it does not have to be spotless. As a result, you can find trousers and jackets from £10. Again this will depend on the quality. Of course, the better the quality, the higher the price.

The advantages of camouflage

This, I would suggest, is self explanatory. The clothing helps you blend in with your surroundings and conceal yourself from your quarry. The other big plus is that genuine clothing of this sort is designed for the sort of activity you will be using it for. It will have been made with consideration of the weather and conditions it was designed for so, as a result, is more than suitable for the field sports arena.

The disadvantages of camouflage

I have already touched on the possible issue of people feeling that the clothing is all they need to have success at their chosen field sport. I do feel that this is becoming a more and more significant issue, especially as we live in a world where the emphasis is very materialistic. I feel it is essential for people to understand that camouflage is a tool that can be used to help you, but that it is not a complete solution or an assurance of success. With the pigeon shooting scenario you firstly, as we have discovered, need to be in the right place and, secondly, you need to be able to shoot accurately. No amount of camouflage can assist your intuition and accuracy, and it is important to understand this.

Another possible disadvantage of camouflage clothing is the way that it is perceived by the public. It is a sad fact that field sports are not widely accepted or understood by those who do not participate in them. Many people hold extremely naïve and biased views with regards to field sports and there is a general misconception about the process and the people who participate in them.

Considering this, it is often something of a shock for a member of the public to stumble across someone who is shooting; they often have no knowledge of what the

Standard DPM camouflage.

person is doing and jump to the wrong conclusion. This is often made worse if the person they have stumbled across looks like an extra from the set of a war film. This is not the fault of the shooter but misunderstandings can arise among town-dwellers. If people stumble across you, whether or not they should be in your vicinity, do what you can to improve the situation. I would suggest removing any facial or head wear, as this tends to help immediately and makes you look more 'normal' than when masked.

Non-camouflage clothing

There is, of course, no written rule that states that you have to wear camouflage clothing to successfully shoot pigeons. Logic dictates that the more concealed you are, the more likely it is that the birds will fly your way without being spooked. The key factor is that if you are shooting over decoys you will be shooting from a hide. The hide, if correctly built, will give you your main concealment so, in reality, dressing in full camouflage is not entirely necessary (at least not if you have built a good hide). Even when roost shooting without a hide, you do not necessarily have to wear camouflage. The key is simply to wear sensible clothing that will blend into your surroundings.

Army surplus clothing is for many the obvious choice. You can find trousers, t-shirts and jackets in a range of browns and greens. This clothing can be ideal as it can look slightly less aggressive than wearing camouflage and it also has the bonus of being designed for outdoor use. The result is clothing that is relatively cheap and comfortable and will also be able to withstand the elements, providing that you get the right items for the time of year. In summer there are numerous lightweight cotton items available. I often by a cheap pair of cotton trousers and spray them with a canvas tent waterproof spray. This turns a pair of normal trousers into a versatile garment that will be light to wear and able to hold off any summer showers. In winter a range of products in Gore-tex, or heavier cotton items, are available. Again, these really do keep the wind and wet at bay. One of my personal favourite items is a heavy parka style coat. This has a removable lining that I take out in summer to give me a light jacket. In winter it goes back in and I am totally insulated.

Surplus clothing is not the only option, and there are many other alternatives available. A visit to most of the major supermarkets can provide you with some basic cheap clothes that can be worn without any worries about getting them dirty or ruined at any major cost. Jeans can be ideal as an all-round item although they weigh you down when wet. With jeans costing as little as £3.00 a pair, can you really go wrong? Again, t-shirts and even jumpers and jackets can be obtained at a small cost and can all prove their worth. A trip to the second hand or charity shop can also prove a worthwhile excursion. I am not a fan of tweed clothing; I find the traditional old tweed jacket is a little heavy and stiff for my needs. Nevertheless, many people do like this style, and the charity shop can be a great place to find such clothing at a fair price. You will also find a wealth of other items and it is amazing at times just what can be found hidden on the end of a rail.

Let us not forget those shops that sell and specialize in outdoor and shooting clothing. Visit most gun shops, country stores and even camping shops and you will find a range of tweeds, moleskins and wax clothing. All of these can be of use depending on your preference. I find moleskin trousers are great for all-round field use, as are cords. They wear well and are generally comfortable in the majority of weather conditions. Wax jackets are a great item for those wet, cold days but they do tend to let the cold in a little. Again, a vast amount of Gore-tex and cotton items are also available and the only limit is the cash you have in your pocket.

DECOYS

Along with a gun and a hide, the decoy is possibly the most important piece of kit for a pigeon shooter. Without decoys you will struggle to pull any birds in, no matter how well you have placed yourself. Decoys have come a long way over the past few years and there is a vast range of different types that can now be used. Traditionally decoys came in two forms. The first was a wooden carved decoy that was painted in the colour of the species being drawn in. The second was to use actual live birds to pull in the intended species. In the case of pigeon shooting, pigeons would have been kept and then tethered out to pull in birds that flew over them. Please note that it is illegal to use live birds as decoys and this must no longer be practised within the UK under any circumstances.

The modern pigeon shooter has three main types of decoy available. There are plastic decoys, flock coated decoys and, finally, the option of using dead birds as decoys. In addition to the actual decoy there is now a range of accessories to which the decoy can be attached. Gone are the days of simply plonking a plastic decoy on the ground. There are now rotary devices that spin decoy birds around to attract the real thing in. There are devices that make decoy birds bob up and down in a pecking motion, and even some that give the indication of a bird flapping its wings. All of these are items that we shall look at as this chapter progresses.

Plastic Decoys

Even with the various modern devices, I do not know of a pigeon shooter who does not own a selection of plastic decoys. Plastic decoys come in two forms; the full-bodied

Full-bodied pigeon decoys.

and the shell. The full-bodied decoy is, as the name suggests, a complete formed decoy that takes the shape of a pigeon. These are secured in the ground by a stake or peg that generally fits under the middle of the decoy and is inserted in a small hole. Full body decoys can be purchased in a range of poses. Some have their head down in a feeding position, others have their heads raised, you can even get some with attachable wings to give the impression of flight. The detail on the decoys does vary but even the cheapest are of a very good quality. A full-bodied decoy is ideal, especially if you intend to use some on lofting poles. The drawback with this type of decoy is that they are somewhat solid and a little rigid, with no play when set in place. Full-bodied decoys tend to cost from £2.50 to £3.50 each, depending on the supplier.

Shell decoys are probably the most commonly used decoy. The shell consists of the top part of the pigeon only. This has a big advantage over the full-bodied decoy in that a dozen or more shell decoys can be easily slotted together and carried in a much more manageable manner than

Shell pigeon decoys.

the same amount of full-bodied decoys. Shell decoys tend to have a small hole in the middle of the decoy. A stake is then secured in this to hold the decoy in place. Shell decoys cost between £12 and £20 per dozen, and they do tend to be sold by the dozen or half dozen rather than separately.

Flock Coated Decoys

Flock decoys can be purchased in the same styles as plastic decoys. The difference between whole-bodied and shell flock decoys comes in the price and, to a degree, the quality. With a plastic decoy, in theory the sun can reflect off the plastic and this in turn could glint and possibly discourage the real birds from flying into your pattern. Flock coated decoys eliminate this as the basic plastic is coated with the soft flock covering. The principle is that the flock stops any risk of glint and thus you have a far more realistic decoy. A dozen flock shell decoys will cost in the region of £16 to £30. Whole-bodied varities will cost

anything from £4 to £7 each depending on the posture of the decoy. Those with wing attachments may be more expensive, and can cost anything up to £15 each.

Feathered / Real Decoys

Firstly, as already mentioned, you must not use live birds as decoys. This is illegal and even if the decoy bird is in theory a 'pet' it cannot be used. By real decoys, I am referring to using shot birds as decoys, and these birds must be dead. You must never leave a wounded bird alive in the hope that it will act as a moving decoy. This is inhumane and illegal. Any wounded birds must be dispatched.

Using shot birds as decoys can be a quick way to add to your pattern with minimal initial outlay. It is totally feasible to start your pattern with half a dozen shell decoys and to add the first half a dozen shot birds to the pattern. The advantage of doing this is that the real thing is naturally going to give off the right signals to those birds in flight. That is, of course, providing they are correctly set out in the pattern. You cannot simply leave a bird where it has fallen and expect it to act as a decoy. You need to arrange any real birds so that they look like feeding pigeons or birds that are flying into the pattern. Again there are a range of accessories that can be made or bought to enable you to do this. The major drawback with using birds that you have shot, especially in the summer, is that they will be useless for eating. The birds will attract flies and will soon become 'blown'.

A useful tip is to put half a dozen birds in the freezer at the end of a day's shooting. These can then be taken out solely for the purpose of using them as decoys on your next outing. They can then be replaced with fresh birds accordingly. Alternatively, if you are talented enough to do so, you could dabble with some basic taxidermy. The idea is that you will skin some birds off and mount the skins to form some decoys. Remember that you are not looking for any museum type specimens. The problem is that doing this is a time consuming process. By the time you have invested in the various chemical treatments needed to treat the skins you could have bought twice as many plastic decoys that would last a great deal longer.

Other Decoys

Over the years, I have experimented with numerous different types of cheap home-made decoys. Most of this was done predominantly in my teens when I was constantly penniless and could not afford decoys. My aim was not to produce great quality 'all singing, all dancing' decoys that would move and sway like the real thing. All I wanted was something that would pull the first few birds in and enable me to then shoot a couple of birds to set out as decoys. The most successful home-made decoys that I could find took two forms. The first was to cut out the basic shape of an aerially viewed pigeon from plywood. This would then be sprayed grey with a couple of black and white spots in the rough location of wings. Finally, the whole thing had a hole drilled in the centre, through which a dowel mounting stick could fit. If you will pardon the expression, they were a little 'wooden' and

A real pigeon being used as a decoy.

Rubber, or flexi-coy, decoys.

Basic decoys gathered together for carrying.

stiff looking but they always pulled in a few early birds that swiftly helped me pull in some more.

The other pattern I used was again to cut an aerial shaped pigeon from grey drainpipe and mount it on a dowel support. This worked just as well as the wooden pattern but did tend to glisten if you did not coat it totally in a matt grey paint. I feel I must add that neither of these patterns worked to the same effect that I have seen real or shop-bought decoys work. That said, using these home-made decoys enabled me to bag enough pigeons to sell and eventually purchase a set of a dozen shell decoys.

Another popular type of decoy from yesteryear was made of rubber and could be purchased in a shell form or as a whole-bodied decoy. The whole-bodied decoy could have a balloon inserted into it and when inflated this gave the decoy its shape and hold. These decoys or 'flexi-coys' work well. They are also easy to bag and carry as, being rubber, they can be folded and packed into a small bundle.

HIDES

The hide is a crucial part of shooting pigeons over decoys. If you have no hide you will be limited in the way you can be concealed, and this will lessen the chances of you managing to shoot anything. A hide needs to conceal you, but you also need to have space enough to keep your equipment and have room to move. Within this section of the book we will look at the different options you have to form a hide. The actual construction of the hide will be covered in a later chapter.

Natural Hides

Before considering anything further, it is possible to make a perfectly adequate hide with natural materials from the area in which you are shooting. All you need is some common sense and some basic tools in the shape of whatever raw materials are available. If you are shooting from the side of a wood then the cover of the trees will give you natural cover from behind. You will then hopefully find a range of fallen branches and foliage that you can use to forge a covering shelter in front of you. This method of hide building is especially relevant in the summer when the ground cover and leaf cover is naturally high. The same principle applies if you are shooting along a hedge or ditch line.

Before using or cutting any natural cover you must firstly ensure that the landowner has no objections to you doing so. Try, if possible, to form a natural hide

in a location where it can be reused. It may even be possible to build a hide in such a way that the natural foliage grows around it so that it becomes part of the landscape rather than a one-off occurrence. This is always an advantage, as pigeons will be naturally wary of any new obstructions, no matter how well they blend into the natural area.

You will often find that harvest time is a very busy time for the pigeon shooter, especially on arable crops such as wheat and barley. The birds will be feeding on any ears dropped on stubble, and good bags can be taken. The problem can be that arable fields are sometimes on the large side. As a result, you can be limited with hide building as you may not have a natural wood line, hedge or ditch to build a hide against. There may not be a single tree that could give you the basics of a hide to build on. One alternative is to ask if the farmer could leave a few bales out in order for you to form a hide. Large round bales can be formed into a triangle or three sides of a square. All you then need to do is produce a front cover and a half roof to shelter you from above. The same can be achieved with small square bales. The likelihood is that you will only need the hide for a couple of weeks and the bales can then be moved and used.

Although not strictly natural, there will generally be a range of items lying around farms that can be used to construct a basic hide. Old pallets or fence posts can all serve a purpose. Likewise, barns and sheds may offer a back coverage or even a useful place to conceal yourself with a minimal amount of hassle. An example of this is a farm that I used to shoot over. In the centre of the farm was a large black corrugated barn. Once inside, the shadows naturally covered you and it was almost impossible to be seen by birds flying towards the barn. Those coming from behind would fly over and drop into the decoy pattern with ease. The whole scenario was added to by shelter from some large oak trees on either side. Finally, it was topped off by a water trough. This area was the easiest I have ever shot from, as you simply put the decoys out, parked the car in the barn and got cracking.

Screen and Netting

Even with using natural resources you may well need to have that little extra to cover an area or perhaps, as mentioned, to cover the front of a bale hide. You could also be in one of those situations when there is very little natural product around, and the result is that you need to construct a hide from scratch. Screen and netting is the ideal product with which to do this, and it can be purchased in a vast range of colours, textures and materials. As you would expect, camouflage plays an important part in this. Screen and netting, as with clothing, comes in both military/surplus patterns and also custom patterns designed purely for field sports.

Screen, also known as mesh, is the most common format on which to find custom designed patterns. This is generally sold in square metres and comes in patterns from woodland designs to marsh style designs (often used for wild-fowling). These screens are made of very small meshed fabric. It is difficult to see into, but you can see out of it as the fabric is not solid.

The view from inside a natural hide that was made in a small wood. Birds were being shot as they flew over the hide to some stubble 20yd away.

The big plus of this sort of hide covering is that it is really light to carry; lengths of 6m or more can be folded and placed in a large pocket.

Camouflage netting is normally associated with military surplus. It is simply a large section of net that has fabric camouflage patterns attached to it. This is generally purchased in three styles; there is the standard green/brown/black pattern, a mixed brown pattern for desert use that is ideal to put around stubble and, finally, a white and green net that is designed for use in snow. This sort of net tends to come in a range of sizes depending on how they have been cut. They are easy to fix into place and long lasting, but they do have one drawback in that they are quite bulky to carry.

Pop-Up Hides

A relatively recent hide that can be added to the pigeon shooter's armoury comes in the form of the pop-up or self-made hide. These again tend to come in the custom-designed camouflage patterns. These hides fold flat for the purpose of transport and are then shaken out and pop into shape. You end up with a complete ready-made hide that you can sit in. The standard design is for such hides to have an entry door in the rear and small windows to the sides and front, out of which you can shoot. These hides are great if you want to eliminate the hassle of having to construct a hide from a net or natural resources.

The drawback is that you have no choice in shaping or making such hides into a custom fit. This may sound impractical but comfort plays a major part in successful shooting from a hide. With a pop-up hide you will be totally stuck with what

you have and this may make them a little cramped or tight if you are of a larger build.

ACCESSORIES

There is a vast range of field sports equipment and accessories that could be of use to the pigeon shooter. One or two items are pretty essential, while others will be of personal preference.

Hide Poles

Hide poles will be essential if you are using mesh or net coverings. Purpose-built hide poles are generally sold in packs of four and these cost from £40 upwards. The basic design will consist of two parts to the pole. There will be the bottom part and, slotted into this, will be the top rod that can be extended to adjust to the height of your choice. The top of the pole will have a catch, or 'v', to which the net or screen is attached. The bottom will be pointed, ideally with a screw style fixing that can

Setting a hide pole securely in place.

A cradle with a bird set in it.

be drilled into the ground. Remember that you will often be setting these poles into rock hard ground so it is crucial that they can be fixed into place without too much hassle.

Alternatives to hide poles can be found in either fishing bank sticks or extendable washing poles. Bank sticks are very similar in design to hide poles, the only real difference comes in the fact that they are often slightly cheaper to purchase. Extendable washing line poles are a great option and can be purchased at a much cheaper price. You will have to make a few alterations, perhaps to the colour and also to add a point, but aside from that they are ideal. Over the years, I have used everything from hazel sticks and bamboo to custom-made metal hide poles. Wooden poles are great on soft mud in the winter but are terrible on the rock hard summer ground. Metal poles will certainly fix in the ground but the drawback is that they are rather heavy to lug around.

Decoy Accessories

We have spent plenty of time assessing the various decoys, and I feel the time is now right to look at what items can be used to enhance your decoys for the best effect. The first thing to understand is that no amount of gimmicks and gadgets can make up for having your decoys in the right sort of pattern. The second point to digest is that decoys will only work if the pigeons are in the area; no amount of decoys will pull in non-existent pigeons.

Cradles, Rockers and Flappers

Cradles and rockers are designed to hold birds that have been shot. The idea is that you place the body of the bird into a supported frame that is raised off the ground. The bird's wings can then be opened and secured in place usually by two supporting metal rods. This gives the impression of a bird rocking with its wings open as if it was about to land. Two or three of these placed strategically can work a treat.

Cradles and rockers can be purchased ready-made from most field sports suppliers. Alternatively, they can be made easily at home with the use of some heavy duty wire and some plastic guttering or an empty bottle. As long as the item used to support the weight of the bird is strong enough to do the job, you really cannot go wrong. A piece of metal rod or dowel can be used to raise the cradle off the ground.

The cradle differs slightly from the rocker, as it is designed to hold the bird with the wings left flat. The idea is that the dead bird is held to look like a bird that is sat feeding. Flappers are very similar to rockers but the bird is normally held at a much greater height. The idea of a rocker is that it gives the indication of a bird about to land and gently flapping its

An empty cradle.

A pigeon rotary device in use.

41

A home-made pigeon flapper.

wings as it comes into land. This differs from a flapper, which gives the indication of a bird already landed and bringing its wings to a close. All of these devices are great pieces of equipment, whether they are home-made or shop-bought.

Springs

One handy tip with regards to shell decoys is to purchase some small springs from a car accessory or hardware shop. These can be fitted on the top of the decoy's support stick and then attached to the decoy. These make the decoys gently bob up and down, making them look that little bit more real than if they were static. Another alternative that a very good friend of mine uses consists of some dowel and hacksaw blades. The design is a simple one and consists of a dowel support rod, attached to which is the hacksaw blade that is cut to a length of about 6in.

A shop-bought pigeon flapper.

A flapper set with a plastic decoy resting in place.

On the top of this is a piece of wood with a hole drilled in the centre of it. This hole can be used to attach another piece of dowel to increase the height to which the decoy can be raised. The saw blade is strong enough to hold the whole device in place, but also springy enough to give the decoy some movement.

Mechanical Devices

In recent years pigeon shooting has taken a new twist with the appearance of rotary devices. These devices tend to run off a small, sealed battery unit. The principle is that between two and four metal arms extend from a central, powered motor. Either purpose-made flock coated decoys or real birds are mounted onto the end of each arm (a cradle principle is generally used). The motor then spins the decoys round at just the right speed to give the impression of birds in flight. These devices have been credited for many a large bag of pigeons and, if used correctly, they can truly enhance a decoy pattern. I do also feel that it is important to point out that if

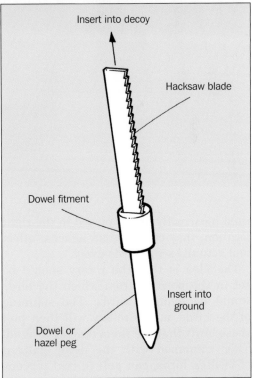

Insert into decoy

Hacksaw blade

Dowel fitment

Insert into ground

Dowel or hazel peg

A diagram of a home-made hacksaw blade spring device.

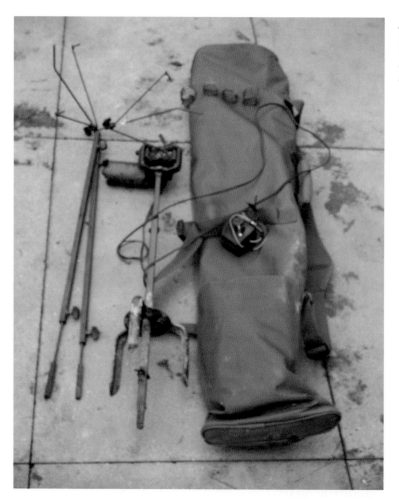

A rotary pigeon device. This model includes two arms that are attached and a speed setting controller.

used incorrectly or not placed in the right location, they can have an adverse affect and actually scare birds away.

The idea is that the rotary should be set in the position from which the birds would be flying inwards. The spinning of the birds on the rotary will then pull those birds that see them moving around. This, combined with the decoy pattern of feeding birds, can pull in real pigeons from some distance. It is also important to ensure that your decoys on the rotary machine are not spinning at a speed that is unrealistic as, again, this will scare away any real pigeons that otherwise would be drawn into it.

Aside from rotary devices, there are smaller mechanical items that are used to simulate a bird pecking. These are generally attached to a single decoy and again consist of a motor that runs on a basic mechanism. These pecking decoys do look impressive as their plastic or flock heads bob up and down, but I am not convinced that they pull birds in any better than decoys set on springs or cradles. To put their worth into context, the rotary devices cost in the region of £70 upwards, and the cost is, I feel, justifiable as they do work. The pecking devices cost from £15 to £25 each, and personally I do not feel that the expense for one of these is something I could justify.

An alternative to buying either a rotary device, a 'pecker' or a 'bobber' is to create your own. I am no mechanical wizard but even I have managed to grasp the basic concept of making one. First, you need a sealed battery, which you can buy from most field sport shops or model shops. You then need a window wiper motor from pretty much any sort of car. Lastly, you need the mechanical ability to attach the motor

to a couple of arms that will hold the decoys.

Calls

The final item that I feel we can class as a decoy accessory is the pigeon call. This is a whistle that when blown is designed to give the impression of the 'coo, coo' call of the pigeon. There are various types available on the market and prices range from £5 to £15. I have not had any genuine success with these items, and have never managed to call any pigeons into a decoy pattern with such a device. I have found them to be of use when roost shooting, especially at drawing birds in that have roosted in trees just out of range.

A crow call, also used for calling rooks.

The secret to success when using these calls seems to be to practise, practise and practise some more until you get the tone and pitch just right. As with the rotary device, if you make the wrong sort of call and do it too fast or too slow it will have an adverse affect and will scare any real pigeons away.

Such calls are also available for corvids and I have to say I find that these work with great effect, particularly with pulling crows and rooks into decoy patterns. Corvids will often circle continually around decoys, each circle pulls them a little closer inwards until they finally come into range. If you are well concealed and you use the call with effect, the birds will actually answer your call. One point that I feel I should clarify in relation to calls is that you cannot use a recording of calls to draw in birds. This is not legal and, aside from the legality, it is considered a somewhat bias approach to decoying. It is one thing to use your skill on a whistle to draw your quarry in and another to whack on a recording that does the job for you.

Bags and carrying devices

You will need some method of carrying any birds that you shoot, and also your decoys and hide poles and nets. On top of this you will need to carry any food and drink you have with you along with ammunition and your gun. The easiest way to transport a gun is in a slip. These are readily available and come in numerous designs and colours. A standard slip will be padded on the inside and have a zipped case with side handles and a shoulder strap. You can buy slips that are extremely basic and do not have any padding or protection apart from the canvas cover. You can also buy leather slips, and some that I have no doubt would cost more than my actual gun. The price you spend on a slip will depend on the quality but they can cost from £10 to over £200.

You may also choose to transport your cartridges in a purpose made cartridge bag. These again come in a range of shapes and sizes. Generally they will hold 50–125 cartridges. Cartridge bags cost between

Various cartridge bags, a cartridge belt, and a range of cartridges.

Two sets of complete pigeon shooting decoys, nets and seats fitted into two army kit bags in the back of the car.

£20 and £50 depending on the quality and size of the bag. An alternative to a cartridge bag is to store your cartridges in an old ammunition storage box. These come in tin form with an easy to open catch, and can be purchased in a range of sizes from most army surplus stores. A good option can be to store your cartridges when in transit in such a box. You can then transfer some to a bag as required.

A general bag for transporting your decoys and nets can be easily constructed by purchasing an army kit bag. These bags are long and deep and, as a result, can be filled with all of your decoys and nets. An excellent idea that I know many, including myself, use is to fit a hollowed out metal or thick plastic drum into the bottom of the bag. You can then place your decoys inside this and your nets on top. When you empty your decoys out and set your nets you can then use the empty drum as a seat. An alternative is to use a purpose made mesh bag to carry your decoys and nets in. These bags are designed for the

purpose and can hold several decoys but when empty will fold down to nothing and fit into a pocket.

You will also need to consider how you are going to carry any shot birds back with you. Another consideration, especially during the summer, is the heat and the flies that will be attracted to any shot produce. You could use another kit bag, or even a mesh bag to hold your shot quarry. In the kit bag the danger is that the birds will sweat and become ruined. A mesh bag is ideal, but if the meshes are not tight (like mesh curtains) flies will still be able to land on them and will lay eggs on the meat. My personal preference comes down to two types of bag. The first is a good old Hessian sack. These can be purchased at garden centres and pet shops and are ideal as they tend to keep any birds stored in them cool. I also find a great deal of use in bags for frozen food, which can be purchased at the supermarket. These will seal shut and are designed to keep frozen food cold, hence their ideal use for storing shot pigeons.

A doubled-up fishing bait box / seat used to store equipment in and to sit on in relative comfort.

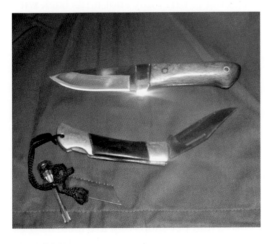

Two knives custom-made by the author. The top is a one-piece bushcraft knife with an ash handle. The second is a folding knife with a buffalo horn handle.

Finally, do not forget a method of carrying your hide poles. An old gun slip or fishing rod bag is ideal. There is nothing worse than trying to clamber over fences and through hedges with your hide poles falling all over the place.

Seats

This may sound strange but to me a seat is the most important piece of equipment after the hide and decoys. I cannot express how uncomfortable it can be to be squashed in a hide for several hours without having something comfortable to sit on. By far the easiest option is the one described above, with the seat forming part of your carrying equipment. This can be further enhanced by placing a block of foam on top of the seat so you have some extra padding. For more comfort, a fishing bait bucket is ideal. If you get two of different sizes you can alter the height of the seat as you choose.

An alternative style of seat comes in the form of the fold-up tripod seats that can be purchased from camping or outdoor shops. These are cheap to buy and do the job, but be warned that the legs can tend to sink into the ground if it is soft. A more expensive alternative is the fold-up 'director' style chair, or a similar version that is often used by fisherman. Again, these are great but the big issue that I have had with these is that they are a little on the large side and they are also a bit too comfortable. The problem with these chairs is that you tend to sink into them. The result is that it can be rather problematic to then move to shoot, especially if you like to shoot standing as opposed to sitting.

A selection of cutting tools ideal for hide building.

Cutting Tools

I would advise anyone who participates in field sports to carry a knife of some description. This does not have to cost the earth, nor does it have to be some fancy, branded tool. It simply needs to be reliable and sharp. A small folding pocket knife will suffice for most tasks and can be purchased from as little as £5. My preferred tool is a sheath knife that is based around the 'bushcraft' design. This is a rugged tool with a chunky blade that is ideal for cutting, skinning and clearing.

Another consideration, especially when you need to clear an area to build a hide or perhaps cut material to form a hide, is the need for a more substantial tool. A small hand axe, a machete or a bow saw would all be ideal pieces of equipment for the pigeon shooter to carry. I appreciate that all of this is yet more stuff to carry. However, there is nothing more annoying than needing to remove a dead branch or a little cover and having nothing to do it with. It is, I feel, far better to be prepared than to be left wanting and maybe even having your shooting hampered thanks to a badly placed twig. It is also rather tedious to find yourself sitting in the middle of a bed of viperous stinging nettles and to have nothing to clear them with. After many years of using all sorts of items, I recently found what I feel is the ideal tool for the pigeon shooter to carry. It is a metal retractable handle that has a spade end. This can be replaced with an axe head that comes with the product and is held in a canvas case. Finally, the handle is hollow

A machete being used to clear cover around a hide location.

and holds a knife blade and saw blade that can also be fitted to the handle. This tool fits onto my belt and covers me for pretty much every possible circumstance.

The final point regarding cutting tools is one of common sense. Nevertheless, it is one I cannot afford not to mention. We live in a culture where, sadly, knife crime is increasing. Therefore, it is imperative that you remember that you must use your tools wisely and that you must not carry them in a public place. Always ensure you secure any knives and keep them out of sight when travelling. Also, always remember to remove any knives or tools from your person if you stop for petrol or at the shop.

Sundries

It is always sensible to take a small first aid kit with you. Try to find one that includes bite and sting treatments. These days a small kit can be purchased from £2 to £5 and this will hold all the basics you need. I carry a large kit in the car and a small pocket sized kit when I am out and about in case I need it.

It is also easy to forget that, when shooting from a hide, you may be out for several hours. In the summer time it can be tediously hot and, although you will be in the shelter of a hide, you will require something to drink. It is very easy to underestimate how much you will need, to take a can or two and to find it gone in a matter of minutes. Cans and small bottles are also yet more to carry. I therefore opt to take a couple of large bottles of water. These will be sufficient for both me and my dog. In the summer I put these in the freezer before hand so they stay nice and cold, they can then be stored in one of my empty pigeon sacks so that they stay cool throughout the day. Food is another consideration, but is one that I feel comes second place to liquid consumption. Finally, if you are shooting on a bright sunny day, you may want to take a pair of sunglasses. Just ensure these are anti-glare so that they do not glint and scare the birds away.

Binoculars can also be a useful item to carry with you, or to have on the dashboard of the car. It will make scouting around a lot easier than having to squint into the horizon, and they can be purchased for a relatively cheap price if you want something basic.

Vehicles

Some consideration should be given to the sort of vehicle that you will have for the purpose of your sport. Ideally, a 4×4 is the ultimate solution. It will allow you to drive almost anywhere to deposit your kit, and gives you much more vehicular freedom than a standard car or van. The main issue with a 4×4 is the running costs and the justification as to whether you really require one. Of course, it would be ideal for your sport, but will it also be ideal for all the other aspects in your life? If you can only afford to run one vehicle it may

Small bag holding mixed essentials including, knives, binoculars, first aid kits and numerous other items.

well not be practical to own a 4×4. Please do not feel that you must have one to succeed at your sport.

If you are considering buying a 4×4, make sure you choose one that fits your requirements and your budget. If, like me, you intend to use it purely for transport when out shooting then do not spend a fortune on some top of the range 'all singing, all dancing' car. I run a small Suzuki jeep, which is ideal for my needs; it is lightweight and, being a 1.3-litre, it is cheap to run, tax and insure.

Dogs

I will confess to feeling somewhat uncomfortable about including dogs in a section of a book that centres on equipment. However, I believe a dog is of far more value than any piece of equipment that you may own. It also needs more care than a plastic decoy or a rusty machete. Accordingly, I needed to cover the topic of dogs somewhere and here was as good a place as any.

In my opinion a dog is the most valuable companion that anyone who participates in a field sport can have. Of course, it does help a great deal if the canine is well trained and has a good relationship with its owner. A dog of any breed does not simply come 'out of the packet' ready to work. It needs to be taught how to do the tasks that it needs to perform. For the purpose of shooting this will normally encompass the following:

- Basic obedience – sitting/staying/recalling
- Retrieving
- Flushing

In addition to all of this, the dog will also be taught to follow hand signals and whistle signals indicating which direction it should go in. The level at which this is taught will greatly depend on just how well you want the dog to perform. If you are using your dog for rough shooting only, this does not give an excuse not to train it properly. It still needs to handle and do things as it is instructed. However, it may not need to do this to the same level as a dog being used for field trials or competitions. For the purpose of this book let us assume that the dog is being used solely for pigeon shooting. You will therefore need to consider the following factors in relation to the training and development of your canine:

- When shooting from a hide the dog will need to learn to wait patiently.
- It will be imperative that the dog does not leave the hide to retrieve unless instructed to do so.
- A dog with the ability to hunt through cover (standing crops and woodland when roosting) will be required.

With the above considered, you should also think about the time it will take to train a dog, and also that when training you will have problems and issues that arise along the way. No dog is perfect and things will go wrong. I am of the belief that a dog of any breed takes at least eighteen to twenty-four months to reach a good level of maturity and work with any effect. It will then be at its peak between five and seven years, with retirement generally following at ten to twelve years. Therefore, you will, if all goes well, have your canine companion for several years – perhaps a decade or more. In that time you will have to feed it, house it and ensure it is kept in good health.

The author's lurcher retrieving a shot bird from the decoy pattern.

All of this comes at a price and, before even considering getting a dog, you must consider if you are able to afford to do so financially.

In addition to the financial side, you also need to consider if you can afford to keep a dog from a personal angle. It is all very well to think that you must have a dog to assist you in your sport. In fact, as stated, I feel it is almost a necessity, especially in relation to retrieving wounded game. However, there is no point getting a dog if you cannot invest your time in it. It will need walking, attention, grooming and stimulation. If you are at work more than you are at home then you may well not be able to give it everything it needs. Likewise, if you have a very active social life that sees you out more than you are in, you may also want to seriously consider whether a dog is something you can really justify obtaining.

Breeds

I do not have the time within these few chapters to go into great lengths over different breeds and training techniques. What I can do, however, is give a brief outline of the breeds that I feel would be most suitable for the pigeon shooter.

Labradors The Labrador is probably one of the most recognizable types of gun dog within the UK. It is a great retriever and is often used for the purpose of picking up on game shoots. Generally the breed will be steady although, like any breed, can be headstrong at times.

Spaniels There are several different breeds of spaniel but the two that I feel are most relevant to us are the springer and the cocker. The latter is of a smaller stature than the first and a little less 'keen'. The cocker is a great dog for flushing and

Shown here returning after picking a runner for a neighbouring gun, lurchers are very versatile dogs.

retrieving, and the breed has increased within shooting circles over the past decade or so. The springer spaniel is a very headstrong breed and one that needs a firm hand to keep it in check. They can be hard work to train and develop, but if you get it right you can have an extremely effective all-round dog. Spaniels tend to be a little more spirited than Labradors when it comes to entering cover.

Mongrels Mongrels come in pretty much every shape and size imaginable. One of the best crosses that I have come across, especially for rough shooting, is the collie × Labrador. This cross seems to live to please and the collie influence gives the dog a real zest when it comes to entering cover.

Lurchers are in effect a breed on their own, but technically they are mongrels so they are not recognized as a breed. The stereotypical lurcher is the greyhound × collie or greyhound × Bedlington or perhaps running dog cross. The lurcher is primarily associated with the pursuit and catching of furred game (since the introduction of the Hunting Act 2004, this now limits the chasing and catching to rabbits and rats) but as a breed it has many more genuine functions. The way a lurcher performs will depend on the sort of cross that it is made up of. Again, within these pages I cannot write reams on this subject. What I can say is that lurchers consisting of part gundog, part running dog and part terrier can be great companions for the pigeon shooter.

CHAPTER 3

GUNS AND SAFETY

Safety is the most important factor in sports that involve shooting of any type. The safety aspect should, I feel, be accompanied by a good understanding of the law surrounding the use of guns and also in relation to the quarry you intend to shoot. Ignorance is no excuse and this should not be forgotten, especially when a gun is being used. You must also remember that a gun in itself is not a danger. To be a danger the gun needs to be operated; it is the handler of the weapon that is the danger and you must never forget this. However, gun safety covers much more than just the use of a gun when actually shooting it. You also need to know how to transport it, store it and carry it in a safe manner. This will not only ensure that those around you are protected, but also that you are kept out of danger.

This chapter explores such aspects as safety in the field and the legalities in relation to owning a gun, whether it is a firearm, shotgun or air weapon. The different guns that you will encounter can be broken down into categories. In order to aid a clear understanding of gun usage and safety, the three categories that this chapter will cover are: the shotgun, the airgun and the live-fire rifle. Having covered the three types of guns, the chapter will close with a short discussion of gun care and some advice on how to obtain permission to shoot.

THE SHOTGUN

A shotgun is defined by the Firearms Act 1968 as 'a smooth-bored gun with barrels of not less than 24in'. Shotguns come in five different styles, these are: the over

A side-by-side .410 shotgun and a 12 bore over and under shotgun.

and under, the side-by-side (both known as double-barrelled shotguns), the pump action, the semi-automatic and, finally, the single barrel. The over and under design is exactly what the name suggests. The gun consists of two barrels one mounted on top of the other. The side-by-side, again as the name suggests, consists of two barrels mounted next to each other or side-by-side. Both the side-by-side and over and under operate in a similar manner.

The gun will consist of three removable parts for the purpose of cleaning and possibly transportation. There is the stock, the barrels and the fore-end. Within these components there are several smaller parts that are all vitally important. The chamber is the area between the stock and the top of the barrels. This is the area that the cartridges will be loaded into. To insert a cartridge, the gun chamber must be opened, allowing the barrels to drop downwards. This is known as a drop down mechanism. You will also have a catch situated on top of the chamber area or possibly on the side of the area. This enables the gun to be opened, and then securely locked when closed.

Most of these styles of shotgun will have a safety catch fitted. In fact, it is only extremely old models that will not be fitted with a safety catch. There are two types of safety catch; the automatic and the manual. The automatic sets itself when the gun is closed so that the gun is 'made safe'. The manual needs to be physically set. It is crucial to note that a safety catch must

A view of a side-by-side 12 bore showing the top mechanism and the barrels and chambers.

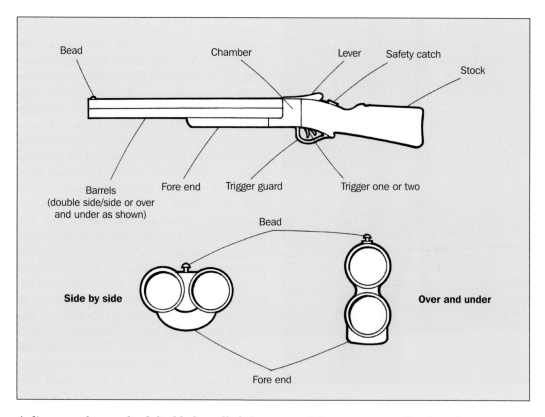

A diagram of a standard double-barrelled shotgun and the components that form it.

never be relied upon; it is an extra port of security and not foolproof. To operate, the gun will be worked by an action. The action consists of firing pins, the safety catch and the trigger. When the trigger is pulled and the safety catch released the firing pins pull forward and connect with the part of the cartridge that holds the 'primer' for the shot. The action may also consist of an ejector system. This means that the cartridges will automatically be lifted from the chamber when the gun is open after firing.

Pump action and semi-automatic shotguns work in a slightly different manner. They do not have a drop down action and, although they can be stripped down for cleaning, they normally operate in a single piece. The cartridges will be loaded into the gun by inserting them into the chamber that will normally have an opening under or on the side of the gun. The cartridges will be expelled from the gun via a gas-propelled or spring action on a semi-automatic gun that also reloads a new cartridge from the chamber. On the pump action a sliding mechanism is 'pumped' by hand to release, expel and reload a new cartridge. These styles of shotgun still have safety catches, but hold a slight advantage for the pigeon shooter because they can hold three cartridges as opposed to the two cartridges that an over and under or side-by-side can hold. It

A bolt action .410 close up.

should also be noted that semi-automatics and pump actions can be purchased with chambers that hold more than three cartridges. A shotgun that holds over three shots is classed as a firearm and a firearms certificate, rather than a shotgun certificate, will be required to own one.

Single-barrel shotguns are curious guns that seem to be somewhat out of fashion. This is mainly due to the fact that they only hold a single shot. The single action will often have a drop down action but sometimes goes a step further in that the gun will completely fold in half. These folding guns were the favourite tool of the poacher who could conceal one with ease in a coat. They were also popular with gamekeepers who could carry them easily while out on their rounds. As well as the drop down single barrel, the bolt action is also relatively common. The action and mechanism is partly held in the chamber, and partly in a bolt that is inserted into the chamber.

An automatic shotgun in comparison to an over and under shotgun.

Some single-barrel guns, and indeed older model double-barrelled guns, may be operated via a hammer action as opposed to the modern alternative that holds the safety catch. To operate the gun the hammer has to be cocked. When released, it connects with the firing pin that activates the cartridge.

Calibre and Choke

The calibre of a shotgun is determined by the number of spherical lead balls that can be fitted into the interior diameter of the barrel. The balls are perfectly shaped, and the total number of balls will make up 1lb in weight. As a result, a 12 bore holds exactly 12 balls, the 20 holds exactly 20 balls and so on. The calibre works in reverse, so a 12 bore is a larger bore than a 20 bore. The most common bores of shotgun are the 4,8,10,12,16,20 and 28 bore. There is also a smaller bore known as the .410. The 4, 8 and 10 bore will not be the ideal choice for the pigeon shooter. The larger bored shotguns are used predominantly by wildfowlers who need guns with large bores to reach the high-flying geese and duck.

The 12 and 20 bore are by far the most common bore of shotgun for use as general guns for shooting vermin and game. The 16 bore is gaining in popularity but is still rather uncommon. The 28 bore and the .410 are also on the up and are often the first choice of calibre to introduce a youngster to. Both of these calibres have hardly any recoil compared to the 12 bore, hence their suitability for use by a beginner before advancing to a 20 bore or a 12 bore.

As well as the calibre, the choke of a gun also plays an extremely important role. A shotgun cartridge is filled with small lead

A hammer action .410 with the hammers visible and the distinctive double trigger mechanism.

balls that make up the shot. The number of balls will depend on the shot size, and the way in which they are spread from the gun will depend on the choke of the gun. Choke affects the way that the pellets are released from the barrels and the pattern in which the pellets are spread. The tighter the choke, the tighter the pattern of the pellets will be. Choke starts from what is known as one-eight choke or improved cylinder. The level of choke then moves in quarters with full choke being the tightest choke possible. If a gun has no choke it is said to be of 'true cylinder'. Many modern shotguns come with choke adjusters so that the choke can be altered depending on the type of quarry or target. For the purpose of pigeon shooting you will be best suited to having a loose choke. This will give you a wider pattern, which serves two important aspects. Firstly, the spread of the pattern will mean that there will be more pellets in a wider area that will connect with your quarry. Secondly, if you shoot with a very tight choke the concentration of the pellets will be so intense that the bird may be hit a little too hard to be of an edible quality. Remember that pigeons are small birds; it only takes one pellet to connect with a vital organ to kill the bird.

To test the pattern and choke of a gun, the common practice is to use what is known as a pattern plate. This will be a flat, metal target. It could be square, round or even cut in the shape of a pheasant or pigeon. The plate will be painted white and set in front of a backstop that will also be white and metal. Shooting at the plate from different distances will show you how tight the pattern is and how many pellets hit the target.

Shot Size

Shot size is another important aspect that should not be overlooked. Shotgun cartridges are loaded with different sized shot and are also loaded with different amounts of charge to ignite the shot and fire it. Shotgun cartridges come in different lengths, and range from 2in (50mm) to 3in (76mm). It is important to ensure that your gun is chambered to hold the cartridges that you intend to use. Most standard 12 or 20 bores will be chambered for a 2½in (65mm) load (please note that other bores, such as the 8 or 10 bore, may take larger cartridges). A shorter length of cartridge can be fitted in a chamber that is longer, provided the chamber is for that calibre cartridge. A longer cartridge cannot fit in a smaller chamber and it is important to remember this. It is also imperative to ensure that you buy the right calibre of cartridge for the right bore of gun. You should also never mix cartridges of different calibre, especially 20 and 12 bore cartridges. Twenty bore cartridges

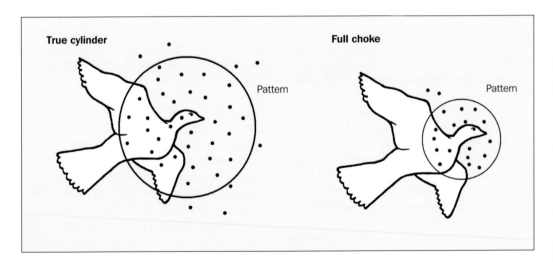

The difference between a true cylinder and full choke pattern.

will fit into the barrel of a 12 bore and will slip down, allowing a 12 bore cartridge to be fitted above it. If this is then fired, the barrel will explode and serious injury can and will occur.

As stated, cartridges are loaded with different amounts of shot. The amount of shot, or pellets, in a cartridge depends on the size of the shot loaded. Shot size is numbered and starts from 1 and finishes at 9. It is worth noting that there are larger shot loads that are recorded in letters instead of numbers, although these are of no relevance for the pigeon shooter as they are by far too large a shot size for pigeon shooting. The more shot there is in a cartridge, the more pellets the cartridge holds. Shot sizes of 1–4 are generally associated with wild fowling and fox shooting. Shot sizes of 5–7 tend to be good all-round loads for game and pigeon shooting. Sizes above 7 are generally used for clay shooting rather than live quarry. One extremely helpful factor is that most cartridge manufacturers now actually produce loads specifically for pigeon shooting. In reality, it is simply a case of ensuring that you have the right size of cartridge for your gun and also that you find a cartridge that you are happy with and comfortable using.

In addition to shot size you should also consider the make up of the cartridge with regards to whether it has plastic or fibre wadding. The wadding is the inner part of the cartridge that holds the shot, and it is propelled with the shot. Plastic wads will not biodegrade well and, thus, can pose a hazard if eaten by stock. Fibre wads will biodegrade and are now preferred mainly because of this factor.

Shot is also loaded in a range of materials, the standard being lead shot. Wildfowl in Britain can only be shot with non-toxic

A selection of spent 12 bore and .410 cartridges.

(non-lead) shot. In other parts of the UK you cannot shoot over wet lands with lead shot, and must use non-toxic shot regardless of the quarry. Lead is the standard shot that the pigeon shooter will use, but alternatives include steel or tungsten matrix shot. Steel costs the same per cartridge as lead does but it has had a mixed reception within shooting circles. Lead tends to penetrate the target and, given its soft texture, will then not ricochet off from the targets and into the surrounding area. Steel is more dense and will at times pass through a target, but it can ricochet. Tungsten matrix is much more expensive than steel and lead and provides the best of both worlds.

Shooting with a Shotgun

In principle, shooting with a shotgun should be an extremely easy task. As you will now be aware, the cartridge ignited by the gun sends a certain amount of lead shot towards the target. It is possible that only one of those balls of shot needs to

A shotgun being held while broken.

A shotgun being held upwards prior to shooting.

connect with the target, so surely missing is impossible? Of course, in reality it is all too easy to miss and the key, as with all sorts of shooting, is accuracy and precision.

To have any success with a shotgun you first need to establish the correct range within which you can be confident of killing the quarry. You then need to develop the correct technique to connect the shot with it. The basic principle with a shotgun is that you do not aim. You should concentrate more on pointing in the correct direction and then allow the movement of your body and the gun to do the rest. The principle I was taught was to move, mount and then shoot. I find that, in this manner, the gun becomes an extension of your arm rather than a separate item. At this point I must stress the importance of safety. You should never fire the gun

unless you are confident and positive that the only thing in danger is the target. Be aware of your surroundings and ensure you know of any hazards and obstructions before even mounting the gun.

A shotgun in 12 or 20 bore is most effective at a range of 35–40yd. You will hit targets further out than this but 35–40yd is the recognized killing range for the shotgun of the above bore. The smaller 28 bore and the .410 will have a much smaller ideal killing range (20–25yd), and the larger bore guns will have an increased killing range. You therefore need to establish just how far 35–40yd is before you try shooting with a shotgun. My recommendation to a novice shot is to go and visit a clay shooting ground before attempting to shoot at live quarry. This will help you develop your gun handling skills and also

The correct way to hold a shotgun with the barrels pointing to the ground.

An incorrect stance with a shotgun. The barrels could swing towards a person or object.

show you just how fast a moving target can travel.

When using a shotgun, the gun should be held in the 'broken' or open position, or with the barrels facing upwards or to the ground. Remember to ensure that the barrels do not point towards anyone or anything else, even if the gun is unloaded. When you go to shoot you will firstly connect visually with your target. You then ensure that the shot is safe. You must ensure that there are no hazards in the line of the target. You also need to make sure that you are not firing towards anyone or anything, such as a nearby road or footpath that could be covered by a hedge but still within range. You should not touch the trigger before being totally happy that the shot is safe.

The next step is to move the gun into the position of firing. You will then mount the gun and bring it in line with the target, and finally you will shoot. Again, this may sound easy but the target will, in most cases, be moving. Therefore, if you aim and point directly at it, the shot will end up going where the target was and not where it is now. You therefore need to allow for lead on the target. This means that when you come in line with the target you actually swing the gun slightly in front of it. This should be done in one fluid action and will result in the target flying or running into the pattern of the shot rather than the shot going behind it. The amount of lead given will depend on the speed that the target is travelling at.

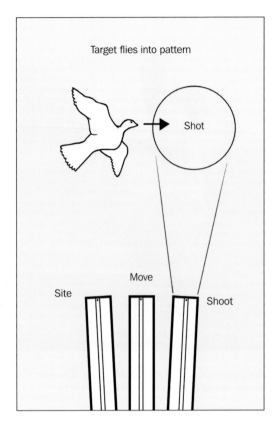

Target flies into pattern

Shot

Move

Site

Shoot

An example of the process of moving, mounting and shooting, while encompassing lead at the same time.

The secret with shotgun shooting is to stay relaxed and to keep focused and positive on shooting and connecting with the target. If you are tense or stressed you are far more likely to shoot in an erratic fashion. The whole process should be done smoothly and unrushed with no unnecessary jerking or jumping around. The pull on the trigger should be smooth and gentle, not quick and tight. When you mount the gun, the stock should fit against the cheek, and your master eye (the eye you use to sight the target) should be looking directly down the barrel top. Most shotguns have beads fitted on the top of the barrel. Do not use these as sights but as guides to point you in the right direction. Also remember that a shotgun does have a degree of kick when it is fired. This means that the gun will move itself when you discharge it. It is important to ensure, therefore, that you have a gun that is of a suitable calibre to your build as, if you do not, you will find it hard to get to grips with the gun. The fit of a gun is all important, and before buying one I would strongly suggest that you spend time enquiring with the gun dealer or gunsmith as to what sort of gun will best suit you.

This leads us nicely to the subject of guns and price, and just how much you can spend. Shotguns come in a vast range of makes and designs. You can pay anything from £100 to over £10,000 for a gun, depending on what you are looking for. The key factor is that, no matter how much a gun costs, it is not going to improve your technique or make you shoot any better. My shotguns are not just used for pigeon shooting, they are general 'tools' used for a wide range of pest control activities. As a result, I have never spent over £200 on a gun. As far as I am concerned, I want something that will last and shoot straight at a fair price. That does not mean that I would not spend much more if I had it to spend in the first place. Gunsmiths and gun dealers will always be able to give advice on what is available for the money you have to spend. Another good tip is to look through the shooting magazines as they often carry reviews or pricing guides to point you in the right direction. Popular makes at the cheaper end include Baikal, Zoli and a number of Spanish and Italian models. Towards the middle to high end of the scale you will find the Brownings, Berretas and AYAs, which are extremely

Moving to shoot after assuring the shot is safe.

Mounting the gun into position ready to take the shot.

The gun is secured to the shoulder and fired at the target.

popular makes along with Moruko, Mossberg and Winchester. The top of the scale seems to cover the shotguns more often associated with game shooting, such as the English game guns of various makes including Holland and Holland.

Shotgun Safety

We have already touched on this to a degree, but I feel a more in-depth look at the safe handling of a shotgun, along with the legal requirement for the usage and ownership of a shotgun, is necessary. Firstly, to own a shotgun you will need a shotgun certificate. This costs £50 and will need renewing after five years (the renewal cost is £40). A shotgun certificate has to be approved and issued by the police. For

them to do this you will need to complete an application form. In addition to the form, the police firearms officer will carry out an inspection of your property before agreeing to issue a certificate. A shotgun certificate is granted under the Firearms Act 1968 Section 2(1).

You will need to ensure that you have a gun cabinet to keep your shotgun in. Most police forces will expect you to have a cabinet before granting a certificate. In addition to this, you should have a secure location where you can keep your ammunition. This should be a dry area that is out of bounds to any children, and neither should it be a location that is in full view of anyone entering or passing your property. The storage of ammunition in this manner is not a legal requirement,

Teaching shotgun safety to the next generation.

but simply good practice. Aside from a secure gun cabinet, some police forces may ask about such things as window locks, door locks and whether or not you have an alarm fitted. Again, the fitting of such extra security items is not a legal requirement, and not something you have to legally have to be granted a certificate.

A certificate can be granted to someone under the age of seventeen provided that their parent or guardian supports the application with a signature. Even though there is no age limit on who can hold a certificate, a person under fifteen may not have an assembled shotgun with them unless they are under direct supervision of someone over twenty-one years old. A person under fifteen may not be given (gifted) a shotgun or ammunition.

A person aged between fifteen and seventeen cannot purchase a shotgun or ammunition, however they can be given, or lent, a shotgun and ammunition. A person aged seventeen can purchase a shotgun and ammunition, and once over eighteen a shotgun can be used unsupervised provided the user has a certificate. An individual who does not hold a certificate can use a shotgun provided they are accompanied by a certificate holder, and are using it with the permission of the owner of the land they are shooting on. Although this may all seem a little heavy on the brain, it is important to be clear on the law surrounding the ownership of shotguns as ignorance of this will not be considered an excuse should you get things wrong.

In addition to the above, you should never carry a shotgun in a public place unless it is securely held in a covering gun slip or case. A shotgun being transported from location to location, regardless if it is by foot or in a vehicle, should also be securely held in a case or slip. Finally, a shotgun should not be left on display in a vehicle, and if it has to be left in an unattended vehicle, the vehicle must be locked and secure.

Field Safety

The above covers the legal aspects and safety aspects of owning and carrying a shotgun in a public place. The next step is to look at the safety of handling a shotgun in the field. The first point is to always treat a shotgun as if it were loaded. If you always treat it in this manner, even when you know that it is unloaded, you will continually respect the gun. Safe gun handling is not something that you need a degree to understand, it is common sense. If you stick to the basics you will not go wrong, whether you are shooting with a shotgun, firearm or air weapon. The basic points in relation to safe gun handling are as follows:

1. **When carrying the gun out of the case always carry it open** unless you intend to take a shot. When taking part in walked up or rough shooting you never know when a shot will present itself. In these circumstances it will be necessary to carry the gun closed, as a shot could occur at any time. If you are carrying the gun in the closed position you should carry it so that the barrels are pointing skywards or towards the ground. Never carry the gun at an angle where the barrels could unintentionally point towards another person or object. If you are carrying the gun closed and pointing to the ground, also ensure it is not pointing towards any dogs or your feet. If you are carrying a shotgun closed you must ensure the safety

67

catch is left on until you need to shoot. If the gun has no safety catch and is a hammer action, the hammers should not be 'set' until the time of firing.

2. **You should never fire a gun at your target unless you are sure** that the direct area that the shot will travel in is safe and clear. The area behind the shot should have a safe backstop that will allow the shot that does not connect with the target to cease its descent. Firing with a shotgun at a flying target is perfectly safe as the pellets will cause no damage when they fall from the sky. You should never shoot at a target when the horizon is not visible or if the target is in a location in which you cannot see around it (such as flying over the brow of a hill or on the skyline). It is important to remember that although the killing range of a shogun is on average 35–40yd, the shot will continue to travel for a further 260–300yd.

3. Always ensure that you have identified your quarry before shooting at it.

4. If shooting with others you should always ensure you know the location of your fellow guns. Never shoot towards your fellow gun or within their ark of fire. The ark of fire is the safe area in which you can shoot without invading your neighbour's space. This is more prevalent with driven game shooting rather than pigeon shooting but should still be observed, especially if shooting with someone in close proximity to you.

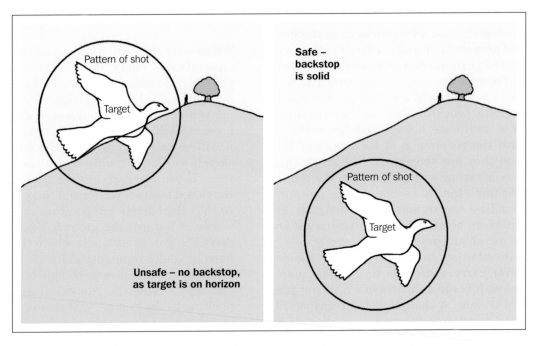

An example of a safe and an unsafe situation when preparing to take a shot.

How not to cross a fence or object with a gun.

5.   Never climb or cross an object with a loaded gun. Always unload the gun before climbing or crossing any obstruction. Place the gun unloaded against a solid object and rest it while you cross over, then pick up the gun and reload. If you are with someone else, cross one at a time and pass the guns between you, but only when unloaded.

6.   Never pass a loaded gun to another person, always unload it and pass it open so that it is clear it is unloaded.

7.   If you drop your gun you should always check that the barrel has not become obstructed. You should also never leave your gun unattended. If you do place it down, try to place it on the flat or lean it securely against a solid object. Never put a gun down loaded, even if it is open.

When crossing a fence alone, lean the gun against a solid object such as a fence. Always ensure the gun is empty before putting it down.

A gun being held correctly in the slip with the fastening at the top of the slip.

8. If carrying your gun in its slip or case, always carry it so that the top of the slip is upwards. If you carry it with the top downwards and the slip is not correctly shut the gun could fall out and become damaged.

AIR RIFLES

The shotgun will be the first choice for many pigeon shooters. The very make up of the gun is ideal for shooting birds in flight. However, there is another aspect to the sport and this sees the use of the air rifle to bag the quarry instead of the shotgun. The two forms of shooting are very different. The shotgun fires pellets from a cartridge, the air rifle fires a single pellet.

Shooting with an air rifle does not require more skill than using a shotgun; it does, however, require a different sort of skill. With a shotgun you do not aim at the target, with an air rifle you do. It is a case of sighting your target, keeping steady and placing your shot in the correct location to drop the bird. The big difference with shooting with an air rifle rather than a shotgun is that you will be shooting your birds when they are stationary rather than in flight.

Different Styles of Air Rifle

There are several different styles of air rifle available. Anyone can own an air rifle providing they are over eighteen years old. You do not have to have a licence to own an air rifle as long as the rifle does not produce more than 12ft lb of muzzle velocity. If an air rifle does produce more than this, a firearms licence is required to own it. Air rifles tend to come in three popular calibres. These are the .22, .177 and .20. There is much debate between 'hardened' air rifle enthusiasts as to what sort of calibre is the best and most accurate. Some swear by the heavier .22, which hits the target with a clout and often imbeds within the target. Others are convinced that the lighter .177 is far more effective. They claim that the pellet travels faster than the .22 and hits with a swiftness that will often see it pass through the quarry. The .20 does not often get mentioned in the debate as it has the best of both qualities. Curiously enough, even with this considered it is the least popular calibre of the three pellets. Personally, I have owned all three calibres over the years and have been more than happy with all of them so have no preference. In my opinion the accuracy lies with the person

An Umarex 850 CO$_2$ rifle, ideal for barn shooting.

pulling the trigger and the provision that the gun, rather than the calibre, is powerful enough to kill live quarry.

With regards to calibre, I would not even consider shooting at live quarry with a rifle with a muzzle velocity of under 10ft lb. Anything less than this will be fine for target shooting but will not have enough power to drop live quarry, with the exception of rats and extremely small vermin. The range of an air rifle with regards to killing will be, on average, 35–40yd. The higher the foot poundage, the more range will be possible. A firearms rated air rifle can have a range of up to and beyond 60yd and can be an extremely effective tool.

Pellets also come in a range of designs and styles. There are some pellets that are sold solely for hunting. There are also flat headed pellets designed for target shooting. The standard pellet has a domed head and in any calibre I find these are ideal all-round pellets.

Airguns in .177 and .20 calibres.

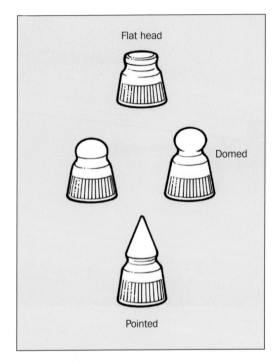

Flat head

Domed

Pointed

Airgun pellets in domed, flat and pointed designs. Others are available but these are the most common.

When the gun is cocked the spring is made tight and is released by the trigger being pulled. The power from the spring compiles the pressure to fire the pellet from the barrel. Most spring-powered guns are fitted with a safety catch. Some will also have built in sound moderators, although the sound from an air rifle is incredibly quiet even without a moderator. It is also commonplace for spring rifles to be fitted with standard open sights. Open sights are basic sights that can be used as a targeting device to prepare for taking a shot. Many open sights will have a small dial that enables you to adjust for range and distance.

Spring-powered air rifles come in three main designs. The break barrel rifle simply has a barrel that is folded downwards to allow the rifle to be cocked and a pellet to be loaded. Under lever rifles have a solid one piece barrel; under the barrel there is a separate lever that is pulled downwards and opens the chamber to allow a pellet to be loaded. A similar but less popular design is the side lever rifle; this works on the same principle but, instead of cocking downwards, the lever cocks sideways.

Although extremely popular, there is one drawback with spring-powered rifles compared to the other types of air rifle. The problem is that the vibration of the spring being released can throw the pellets off slightly. I must add that the gun is not solely to blame for this. It is simply recoil that is being released and if the shooter is holding the gun correctly and prepared for the shot then there should be no issue. We are not talking about a huge variance that will see the pellet missing by inches. The recoil may only throw the pellet off by a fraction of a millimetre but this could make the difference between a kill and a wounding shot.

You will find that your rifle will often suit a make of pellet and perform better with this compared to other brands. I would suggest that you establish the pellet that the rifle likes and stay with it. There are various products that can be bought to help pellets fire supposedly in a more accurate manner. Pellet oils or lubes are used to coat the pellets prior to firing. Personally, I do not find them of any use although they are there if you wish to try them. Air rifles come in three main varieties; the spring-powered, pre-charge and hand-pumped designs.

Spring-Powered Rifles
Spring-powered air rifles, as the name suggests, are operated by a powerful spring.

Shooting with a spring powered airgun.

Spring rifles can be bought from as little as £50 or as much as, and sometimes more than, £400. There are many moderately priced rifles that are more than up to the job but, as with everything in life, you get what you pay for. Popular makes and suppliers include SMK, BSA, Whirwheuach, Baikal and Cometa. Please note, these are not the only suppliers and they are listed purely as examples and not for preference.

Pre-Charged Air Rifles
Pre-charged air rifles are now extremely popular and I would suggest they have overtaken spring guns' popularity over the past decade. The advantage with these types of air rifle is that they do not release any recoil when fired and as a result the only factor that might throw a shot off is the wind or the person pulling the trigger. Pre-charged rifles come in two main styles. The first style sees a small bottle being filled with compressed air. This is then attached to the rifle and removed when it is empty. A bottle will allow for several shots to be taken before it needs refilling. Most rifles will allow for a minimum of 100 shots before the bottle needs recharging. To refill the bottle is a simple process that involves a larger compressed air bottle used to charge the smaller bottle up.

The alternative to the 'buddy bottle', as it is known, is to use a rifle that has the air charge pumped directly into the chamber of the rifle. A large pre-charged bottle can be used to do this or a device known as a stirrup pump can be used. The pump is hand operated and connects to the chamber. A gauge measures the level of the air and tells you when the chamber is full. There is very little difference between the two designs apart from the weight of the rifle. Those with a chamber are slightly lighter than those with a bottle. As with a spring powered gun, pre-charged rifles will also have open sights fitted and safety catches. The big plus with these sorts of rifles is that they will often have magazines that hold more than one pellet. This allows for much quicker firing, especially as most of these guns are bolt operated. The same makes as with spring guns are available but other popular models include Theoben and Air-Arms. The big difference with pre-charged rifles compared to spring powered rifles is the cost. You will not find a pre-charged gun for under £200 and prices can range to as much as £1,000.

There is a third type of rifle that I feel we should mention within the pre-charged section and this is the CO_2 rifle. These are not as popular with those who are seriously into their air rifle hunting. Nevertheless, they can be a good stepping stone from a spring gun to a pre-charged rifle. CO_2 rifles are also constantly improving and can prove very effective for hunting. These rifles run off CO_2 capsules, one or two small capsules are inserted directly into the chamber. Alternatively, a larger canister is fitted directly onto the chamber in a similar fashion to the way a buddy bottle is fitted. Those guns that operate on the smaller canisters will give around thirty to fifty full powered shots. The larger canisters will give from 80–150 full powered shots. I must stress that you will get more shots out of the gun than

this, but these will not always be powerful enough to kill live quarry.

CO_2 guns have two main drawbacks for live quarry shooting. The first is, as mentioned above, that not all of the shots will be powerful enough to kill live quarry. This can be difficult to gauge if you are not used to using this sort of rifle. I have experienced this myself and it took several sessions at targets to work out just how many 'full power' shots I could take. In addition, it is at times tricky to remember how many shots you have fired and if you have enough power left in the gun. This is added to by the variance released from the capsules that alters depending on how hot or cold the gun is. The second drawback is that the capsules and canisters cannot be refilled. As a result, it can prove quite costly to run such guns. The price of CO_2 rifles is considerably lower than both spring and pre-charged rifles, with prices between £80 and £300. The two most common makes within the UK are Crossman and a model supplied by SMK.

Hand-Pumped Rifles

These types of rifles are very much in the minority given their make-up. The gun has an air chamber within it but, rather than filling it with a bottle of air, you physically have to pump the air into the chamber. The hand pump rifle will have a pull down mechanism that when pulled and then retracted will place a charge into the gun. In most cases these rifles will need several pumps put into them for a shot that could kill effectively. The problem is that pumping the charge into the rifle in this manner can be somewhat tiring and if you miss you have to do it all again.

I have a fondness for hand pumped rifles but it would be wrong for me to recommend one as the ideal tool for the pigeon shooter. I own one and use it regularly for rabbit shooting and occasionally for roost shooting. The rifle is very light and extremely accurate but it does take some effort to keep pumping it for a shot. The most common types of pump airgun are the Sheridan and the Crossman. The main plus with these rifles is that they are light and, in my opinion, they are ideal training weapons for youngsters. You can control the charge put in the gun and there is no recoil, and they can be a great tool to use before moving to a pre-charge rifle.

Shooting with an Air Rifle

The big difference in shooting with an air rifle rather than a shotgun is that you will aim at your target. The skill lies in placing the pellet in the right location to kill your quarry quickly and accurately. To do this you will need to develop a steady hand and also learn to use the wind and surroundings to your advantage. With a shotgun you will be allowing for lead when you shoot at a moving target. With an air rifle your target will be stationary.

It is easy to think that you simply just point, aim and pull the trigger, and to a degree this is true. The issue comes with allowing for the wind that will alter the direction, even by millimetres, of the pellet. Therefore, you need to remember this and allow for it when you aim and take your shot. You also need to allow for the angle of the target and the drop of the pellet. If you are shooting at a pigeon sitting high in a tree the pellet will go too high if you aim directly at the bird. You need to aim slightly lower to hit the right spot.

It is all too easy to assume that the best place to shoot a pigeon is directly in the chest. The problem is that the front of the chest is covered in thick feathers and also the crop is situated in the direct centre of the pigeon's breast. If the bird is front facing the best place to aim for is to the left or right of the breast centre. If the bird is side facing then the front curve of the wing as it joins the breast is the ideal spot. Of course, in my opinion the ideal point of aim is for a head shot. This will kill the bird instantly and also leave the meat undamaged by the pellet.

Shooting with a pump powered airgun.

The correct areas to shoot with an airgun to ensure a kill shot.

I am a great believer in learning to shoot an air rifle with open sights at first. I feel this helps to teach accurate shooting and precision. It also helps you to judge range and to learn if you have any natural traits when shooting. By an example of this, I always tend to shoot slightly to the right. I have learnt to compensate for this by aiming slightly more to the left. I identified this issue with open sights. With a telescopic sight it was all to easy to blame the sight and not myself for the issue. Although I feel it pays to learn with open sights, there is no doubt that a telescopic sight will help your shooting no end. You will have a far clearer view of your target and this will aid the chance of a good, clean kill.

A telescopic scope is a magnification device that is fitted to the rifle and enables you to view the target in much more detail. Scopes come in two formats, those with fixed magnification and those with variable magnification. Fixed magnification scopes hold the same image but this can still be zoomed in or out. Common examples of fixed magnification scopes are the 4×20, the 4×32 or the 4×40. Variable magnification scopes can also be zoomed in or out, but have the advantage of being adjustable so that the image can be increased or decreased. With a fixed scope to a 4×32, for example, the image will always be four times the size of the object. With a variable of, say, 3×9×40, the image can be varied from between three to nine times the size of the target.

Scopes vary in price depending on quality, but a scope suitable for an air rifle will be purchased easily between £30 and £100. You could spend more than this but, in all honesty, you will be wasting your money investing in a really pricey scope on an air rifle. At the other end of the scale you could pick up a scope for much less than £30. The problem comes in that some of these cheaper scopes tend to be more liable to wear and tear than the higher value scopes. Remember that there will be some recoil – not least with a spring gun – and this may well alter the scope, especially if the scope is not well made in the first place.

A scope will be fitted with cross hairs that are visible when looking through it, and these are the part of the scope that you will use to sight your target. Your point of aim will be the centre of the cross hairs. In addition to this, a scope has two reticules situated in its centre. One reticule is used to adjust the scope from left to right, the other adjusts up and down. A scope needs to be fitted to the rifle and will not simply sit in place and be balanced for a perfect shot from the gun. It needs to be fitted and then sighted in by using the reticules to adjust the scope to the rifle.

To sight a rifle you should fit the scope to the gun and aim at a target. At first the target should be situated roughly 10yd away. Make sure the rifle is held as steady as you can possibly hold it, then shoot at the target. View the shot and then adjust the reticules accordingly. To adjust, it is normally a simple case of clicking the correct reticules by the amount indicated on the scope. For example, it may be that the shot is 4in off from the centre of your target. The height is correct but it is out to the left. You would therefore adjust the scope to the right by however many clicks were needed. The scope is held in place to the rifle by mounts that clamp the scope to the gun and hold it firmly in place. Some scopes come with mounts, but often you need to buy these separately. Once you have sighted the rifle at 10yd you then

need to sight it at ranges increasing by 5yd each time until you have it zeroed to the distance you intend to shoot at. In my case I zero my rifles to 30yd. I find this gives a good centre range for shooting, with allowances made for shots over or under this distance.

The key to successful air rifle shooting is confidence and concentration, combined with a steady hand. Make sure you keep your breathing paced and remember not to snatch or grab at the trigger. You should gently squeeze the trigger with one fluid motion. There are various stances that can be taken to hold the rifle steady. You can buy cross sticks to rest the gun on in a variety of heights. I use a thumb stick as a rest for the gun. The key is to learn to take the weight of the rifle in the most comfortable fashion for you. It is also important to remember that if you are not shooting from a hide, and are instead roost shooting or perhaps rough shooting for pigeon, the shooting position you need to take will not always be predetermined. All too often it is a case of having to take the shoot there and then. As a result, I would always suggest practising shooting from a range of distances and stances.

A good quality telescopic sight.

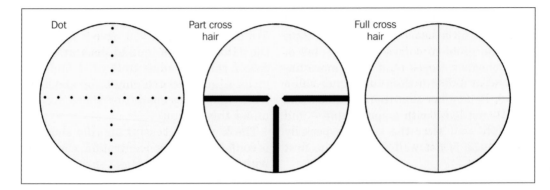

Different designs of crosshairs including dot, part and full cross hairs.

Air Gun Safety and the Law

It is a sad fact that air rifles are often viewed as being less dangerous than live-fire rifles and shotguns. You do not need a licence to buy an air rifle or to own one (unless it is over 12lb ft). As a result, it is easy for airguns to be purchased by individuals who want them for the wrong purposes. Consequently, an Act of Parliament was introduced on 6 April 2007 (The Violent Crime Reduction Act 2006). This act does not just concern air rifles, but has made changes to the law. These are listed below:

- Airguns can now only be sold by a licensed firearms dealer in a trade capacity. Prior to the act anyone could sell or supply them for trade (you can still sell an airgun privately as long as it is not done for trade or business).

- Trade sales must take place face to face and can no longer be done over the phone or by post. The buyer and seller must both be present.

- Airguns can only be purchased by someone over eighteen years old (prior to the act this was seventeen years old).

- It is an offence for an airgun pellet to be fired beyond the boundaries of the land where the user has permission to shoot.

In addition to the above, an airgun cannot be carried in a public place unless it is in a secure case. A person under eighteen years old can use an airgun on private land providing they hold the landowners consent – they must be accompanied by an adult if under fourteen years old. Finally, the act also banned the sale and ownership of a type of airgun that ran on pre-charged cartridges. This part of the act has, at times, caused some confusion and it is important to understand that this does not mean CO_2 or pre-charged rifles. The ban applies to air weapons that operated on a bullet/cartridge system in which the actual cartridge or bullet was charged with air and primed to fire by doing this.

Aside from the above, the usual safety precautions described with shotgun shooting should be put into place when using an air rifle. Although the rifle will have a smaller range than a shotgun, you should always ensure that you have a safe backstop and that you have identified your quarry before shooting. Please remember that an air rifle can still do a great deal of damage. It is feasible that a shot from an air rifle could kill a person. Make sure you treat the air rifle with the same respect you would give any other sort of firearm or shotgun.

LIVE-FIRE RIFLES

Live-fire rifles come in two forms; the centre fire and the rimfire. The centre fire rifle is operated by the bullet being propelled by a centre firing pin igniting the bullet. A rimfire is fired by the rim or edge of the bullet being crimped to fire. In reality, live-fire rifles will not be the usual tool of the pigeon shooter. They are more often associated with the control of ground game and vermin. Large calibre centre fire rifles such as the .243 and .270 are often used for the control of deer and foxes. The .222 and .22 rimfire and .17 are associated with foxes, rabbits and hares.

The main reason that live-fire rifles are used for ground game control is that the bullet released can travel for a much further range than an air rifle pellet and a shot released from a shotgun. A .22 rimfire bullet can travel for several hundred yards and a centre fire bullet can go much further than this. It is therefore essential that you always have a solid backstop. With this in mind, I was always taught, and stand by the opinion, that a live-fire rifle should never be used for an aerial shot or a shot skyward into a tree. The only time I would use a live-fire rifle for pigeon shooting would be to take out corvids that came into the decoys or pigeons on the ground. Even then this would also depend on the ground I was shooting on. The other danger with live-fire rifles is that there is a risk of ricochet if the bullet hits a stone or solid object.

Live-fire rifles can only be owned if you have a Firearms Certificate. If your only sport is pigeon shooting I would suggest sticking to a shotgun or air rifle and leave the live-fire rifles for ground game and vermin only.

GUN CARE

Whether you are using a shotgun, air rifle or live-fire rifle it is important, as with any tool, to look after your gun. With reference to rifles and air rifles, I do not believe you need to clean the inside of the barrel. I find that a rifle shoots straight and accurately if the barrel is left with any residue in it. This of course is my own opinion. A rifle will need an oiled cloth run over the outer side of the barrel and mechanism, especially if it has become wet. It is also worth using a soft brush to wipe some oil over any springs and internal mechanisms. Scopes should be kept clean and lenses given a wipe with a dry, soft cloth if they have become wet.

Shotgun mechanisms and outer metal work should also be cleaned with a soft brush or oiled cloth. You will also be able to break a shotgun down so components such as fore-end levers and the chamber and ejectors can also be cleaned and oiled. With rifles of any form, a bolt or magazine may be removable for cleaning. Additionally, the gun should not be transported or stored with bolts or magazines in place; they should be stored and transported separately. The internal barrels of a shotgun should be cleaned out periodically, especially if the gun is used regularly. A cleaning rod is used that has

.17 and .22 live-fire rifles.

various different end attachments. These include wire brushes, soft cloths and brushes and also a wool brush. These are used to apply oil to the inside of the barrel and to clean and remove any dirt.

You should check your gun after use for any damage or faults. Check the stock and any woodwork for cracks or chips. Check the barrels for any scratches or pitting, and if you do find any faults consider consulting a gunsmith. Any issues can be reduced if you just remember to respect your tool. If it is wet then dry it thoroughly before locking it away. If you keep it in good condition it will serve you well for years. My first shotgun was a second hand Zoli over and under. I used it for years for everything from game shooting to vermin control and pigeon shooting. I would use it for rabbit shooting off the back of a Land Rover, and for shooting bolting rabbits over ferrets. I kept good care of it and finally replaced it after about ten years when it became apparent that getting the firing pin replaced for the fourth time was not a viable option. Likewise, my first proper airgun was an

HW80 with a silencer fitted. This was also heavily used, in fact it was used pretty much daily for about four years before it needed a new spring fitted as the original had become worn.

OBTAINING PERMISSION TO SHOOT

If you intend to shoot pigeon you will need somewhere to pursue them and this will mean obtaining permission to shoot. As we have already touched on when we looked at the Wildlife and Countryside Act, you cannot simply shoot whenever and wherever you choose. You need to have the landowner's consent to shoot on his property. If you do not obtain this consent, you are poaching. In addition to this, if you have a gun with you other offences will also be committed. Poaching may seem a somewhat minor offence to many, but add to this issues like armed trespass or possession of a firearm illegally and things can suddenly become a lot more serious.

There are various ways that you can go about obtaining permission to shoot over land. One is simply to spend some time driving around your area and observing where you see pigeons feeding, or noting crops that could be at risk. You can then note these areas on a map and write to the farmers that own the land. When you write, do not pen a letter that gives the impression that you want to do the farmer a favour by shooting on his or her land. Write a clear, concise letter that states your full intentions, mentioning whether or not you have any insurance and also any previous experience you have of shooting. It is also worth mentioning a little about your background and your intentions with regards to any shooting that may be granted. With your letter, send a stamped addressed envelope. One thing I would say is that if you go about trying to obtain permission to shoot in this manner, you will get more blanks than positive responses and this can be somewhat soul-destroying.

The problem is that there are many other people also seeking shooting, and they may well be doing exactly the same as you. Farmers are busy people and, often, letters from people wanting to shoot can become a little tedious and end up being binned. In addition to this, remember that farming is a business and if farmers have arable crops growing then, more often than not, they already have provisions in place for the control of vermin. Another option is to cold call and knock on farm doors enquiring if there is any chance of shooting. This can have mixed results and I must confess it is not something that I am keen to support. Unfortunately, crime in rural areas does occur and you may well be viewed with suspicion if you turn up unannounced at a farm. If you do decide to take this approach, do not go dressed in your field wear. Dress smartly and try not to be pushy. If nobody is in, do not start poking around the farm looking for somebody; call back another time or perhaps leave a letter in the post box.

Of course, farms are not the only place that pigeons reside. You may in the first instance have more luck by trying to secure shooting on smaller areas of land, such as nurseries or smallholdings. These places may not have vast amounts of birds feeding on them, nevertheless there may be some to shoot that are feeding on the vegetable plot or suchlike. If you can get access to ground in this manner, and prove yourself to be trustworthy and an asset, then the larger areas of ground may follow as your reputation spreads.

An alternative to trying to gain access in these ways is to join a pigeon club. These clubs are a very good idea in principle, and do help many people gain access to ground where, otherwise, they may have never have gained permission. Basically you pay a yearly fee to the club and for this you have access to a vast amount of land. Clubs do vary in the way they are run and operate. In most cases you will have to provide proof of insurance before you can shoot. This can be obtained independently, but most people who shoot receive insurance cover by joining a shooting organization that offers insurance as part of the membership package. This insurance is generally third party and does not cover professional pest control activities, so always ensure the cover you have does what you require of it. The British Association of Shooting and Conservation and the National Gamekeepers' Organisation, along with the Countryside Alliance, all offer very good insurance with their memberships.

Pigeon clubs do give you a great amount of ground to shoot over but be careful not to join one that is flooded with members. Too many guns in a club means that the birds will, at times, be over-shot and you will end up spending many a wasted day out chasing very nervous pigeons. On a safety note, most clubs tend to operate in a way that sees members having to inform the club of where and when they are shooting so that the risk of two guns being in the same place at the same time are limited. There will also be rules within most clubs stipulating that cartridge cases should be picked up and that shot birds are removed from the site. These things are general good practice and should be encouraged within or outside of a club.

Another option to gain shooting is to beat on a local pheasant shoot. In many cases those beaters who prove themselves to be a useful, hard-working part of the shot during the season may well get the opportunity of some shooting of vermin, including pigeons, throughout the year. Beating does not only give you the chance of getting some sport via the estate, you will also meet many like minded people who may be able to help you in your quest for some shooting.

Finally, you could opt to get your shooting by going out with a pigeon guide. These guides will have permission to shoot over thousands of acres of ground, and you pay them to find some shooting for you. They then accompany you out and set up the decoys and hide for you to shoot from. You will also find guides who will simply find the birds and leave you in the required location for the day. This sort of ready-made shooting is not personally something that I would partake in, but I can fully understand why someone would if they had no shooting of their own. The cost of a guide or a day's shooting will vary but will, on average, be in the region of £80 to £160.

With money being mentioned I feel we should look at the possibility of paying for your shooting. If you want to shoot more than just pigeons then you could consider renting some ground to shoot over. This will entail acquiring the shooting rights or tenancy to shoot on land. Although, be warned: if your main quarry is pigeons you should think long and hard before doing this. Most shooting rights are taken out for game shooting. The rights will include permission to shoot vermin but, in many cases, the tenant farmer or landowner will also have permission to shoot vermin to protect their crops and livestock. This works well if the ground has been rented for game shooting, but is not ideal if you intend to only shoot pigeons. If you do pay for your sport, you will need to ensure that any contract stipulates exactly what can and cannot be shot.

CHAPTER 4

SHOOTING OVER DECOYS

We have already looked at the feeding habits of pigeons, along with spotting likely roost spots for use in the day and at night. We have also looked at the all-important flight lines. The next step is, therefore, to focus on the actual process of shooting pigeons over decoys.

THE GROUND WORK

Let us assume that you have already done your homework and have been monitoring the crops that the birds are feeding on. This will depend on the time of year and it could be a crop of freshly sewn winter wheat or rape. Alternatively, it could be summer and the birds may be feeding on flattened patches of cereal crops, or perhaps the fall from the recently harvested wheat, oats and barley. Whatever the crop, you will have kept an eye on the birds and their feeding habits. You will have noted what time they tend to go out to feed and when they return to roost. You will have also spotted the water trough that they congregate around at the far end of the field and the twisted old oak that stands further up the hedge and serves as a daytime roost.

After considering the above, you have also taken into account the three flight lines that span the field you intend to shoot over. You know that, for the best results, you want to set up between the three flight lines with the trough to your side and the tree out of range but in view. In an ideal world a couple of guns would be best suited to covering the field, but on this occasion you are on your own so you shall have to make do. You decide to set up on the field during the late morning. This means that the birds may already have fed early on and, around the time you set up, will be at roost digesting their feed. This will give you time to build the hide and set the decoys so that you are ready to start shooting just after midday. By this time, the birds will just start drifting out to feed. By mid-afternoon the numbers will pick up and they should stay good until late evening when they will finally return to roost. Of course, before setting up you would have notified the landowner of your intentions and ensured that they are aware of your location and the times you will be shooting. You will also ensure that you know the best place to park your vehicle, and if you can use any natural cover to build a hide. When you finally arrive on site and unload your kit, remember to then park your vehicle away from the area you are shooting so that its presence does not to spook the birds.

MAKING A HIDE

Your first job is to build your hide in a suitable location. You want to ensure the direction you are shooting in is well clear of any hazards or obstructions. Ensure

Wooden pallets can be arranged quickly to form the basis of a hide.

that footpaths and bridleways are not in your direct line and range of fire. Make sure that you are aware of any stock grazing and you are not shooting at any other hazards, such as phone lines or power cables. Also remember that it is illegal to shoot within 50m (55yd) of the road side, so if you are shooting on fields close to roads make sure that you observe this.

The location of the hide may be altered from you ideal spot due to the above factors and also the wind direction. The wind plays an important factor with pigeon decoying. The birds like to fly with the wind acting in their favour. They will use the wind to assist them with their flight but once landed will turn so their heads are facing into the wind. Therefore, you must set up your hide so that the decoy pattern allows for the birds to land comfortably, and with the aid of the wind. You will also need to note the direction the birds are flying from, and what angles you intend to shoot from. In most situations the area you intend to shoot will be directly in front of the hide. This will allow you to build the hide with a roof cover to shade you and cover you from above and the 'bird's-eye

view'. This is important as the birds that fly over will pick up on any movement from within the hide. A roof cover will prevent this from occurring. The secret is to build the roof so that it only covers the rear half of the hide. This will still allow you room to shoot forwards and to the side of the hide in a circular angle without having your full view blocked or your swing inhibited.

There will be times when you may not need to put a roof on a hide. One such example would be if you set up with a hedge as your back stop. If the hedge is higher than the front area of the hide a roof will not be needed. The hedge will give you natural cover and also prevent any shots from the rear, so you can focus purely on shooting to the sides and front. Another situation when a roof may not be required – when a hide may not be required at all, in fact – is when you are shooting on the edge of a wood. From time to time you may be lucky to find the birds feeding close to the edge of woodland that gives a natural hide without the need for any tweaking. I have had this on occasion and the bracken and bramble has given me a natural shelter without having to cut a branch. All I have needed is some suitably blended clothing and the ability to sit or stand still when the birds fly inwards. In this situation you will also find that birds will head for the trees and you can shoot a full 360 degrees with ease.

If you are building a natural hide, firstly clear some space where you intend to place your seat and equipment. Make sure you have enough room to be comfortable and you are able to raise and manoeuvre your gun without feeling inhibited. Once you have cleared your space, take the stance you intend to hold while waiting for a shot. You can then build your cover around this at the right height. There are two ways you can build a natural hide. One is to position yourself so that natural cover, such as bramble or elder, can be bent and curved to shelter you. Such cover can easily be weaved and twisted to make a good frontal cover. I say frontal cover because I would only build such a hide if I had a hedge or large tree to my rear to build the hide around. If I did not have this I would be looking to construct a net hide instead of a natural hide. The second method of building a natural hide is useful if you do not have a natural back stop or if the cover is thin on the ground. The key is to use the shade to your advantage and then use branches and foliage to construct a hide that can be aided by the shade and shadows. Such a hide is ideal if you are perhaps shooting in a small block of trees, or in a thin spindle of woodland where natural cover is sparse.

If you are shooting in an area where there is no hedge or cover and the area is heavily exposed, it can be much harder to conceal yourself. If you are shooting on cereal stubbles, by far the best option is to form a bale hide. Ideally this would be a square bale hide that can be left in place. The principle is simple, the hide is formed of bales stacked two high at the back and sides. One bale then stakes at the front to cover you. The drawback is that you are limited to shooting forwards only, unless you wish to continually spring up and reveal yourself. The big plus of bale hides is that if the birds are really focused on one location you can leave the hide in place and use it on multiple occasions. Of course, you must always ensure that you seek the landowner's permission to use bales before making such a hide.

Square bales, especially the small ones, seem to be in decline these days and on many farms you will find the large round bales. These make an excellent backstop for a hide that can then be constructed in front of the bale from net. There are two options to do this. One is to use three hide poles to form a triangular shape that centres towards the decoy pattern. A roof will not be needed as the bale will cover you from behind. You could use four hide poles to form a square hide that has the bale as

Using a fencepost as a starting point, branches and foliage can provide convincing cover on otherwise open ground.

Preparing a spot for a hide after conducting some reconnaissance to ensure things are being set in the right place.

a backstop. This will allow a little more room but some roof coverage may be required.

If you opt to build your hide along a fence line or a hedge line, but intend to use nets combined with or without natural cover, you have several options available. Both the triangular and square design can be used to great effect. If the cover formed to the rear by natural foliage is sparse, use a sheet of netting or Hessian to increase the cover. My personal favourite hide design is that used by my close friend, and it combines the best of a triangular and square hide. The hide is made with three square sides at the same height. A roof cover is then added to these sides. The hide is set on four hide poles, as with a square hide, but then has a fifth hide pole added. This is situated at the front of the hide and the hide is then angled out to this pole. This gives a square area to sit in with a

Attaching the netting around a hide.

triangular frontal area. The advantage of this is that you have an increased area in which to raise your gun and shoot from. It also gives you a good view of the entire area and makes for ideal shooting.

When you build your hide remember to ensure that it has an entrance and exit for you to use in order to collect shot birds. Also ensure that the hide is anchored down well so that it does not blow too much in the wind. As well as your hide poles, a few tent pegs hooked down with bungee cords that attach to the hide poles can be a great extra support. You could also add a few tent pegs to the bottom of the net without the bungee, but from experience this tends to snag and tear the net. In summary you should remember the following when making a hide:

A tent peg being used to secure the net in place with the aid of a bungee cord.

1 Observe the way the birds are travelling before building the hide.

2 Observe the area where the birds are feeding and assess whether or not there is a second feeding spot close by. Accordingly, determine whether or not there is a second area where a hide could be set if the first did not prove suitable.

3 Plan how you are going to make your hide and remember to take into account the distance from the hide to your decoy pattern.

4 Make sure you have a safe area to shoot towards and check for hazards before building the hide.

5 Remember to leave plenty of space for your kit and enough room in which to move when shooting.

Inside the hide with the relevant equipment ready for use.

87

The view from the front of a hide looking outwards to the decoy pattern.

SETTING THE DECOYS

Once your hide is in place you need to set out your decoy pattern. The first thing to establish is the area over which your decoys will be placed. Make sure you account for the sort of gun you are using and do not set the decoys too close or too far out. I would suggest setting the first decoy at around 20yd. The last can then be set at 30yd. This will give you a good range to shoot in and will also be far enough out to attract the birds inwards as they fly round and over the pattern.

You must take into account the natural lay of the land before placing the decoys out. There is no point setting them if they are in a location that will hide them. Such areas could be in small valley dips or too close to the shade of a hedge or wood line. The decoys must be visible and must stand out to have any effect, and you also need to make sure they are visible above any standing crops. There is no point setting decoys in tramlines if the crops are standing 2 feet high – the decoys will be completely covered and not visible even from the air.

The most common decoy pattern is the 'horseshoe'. This, as the name suggests, is when the decoys are set out in a semi-circle. The circle must be large enough to funnel the flying birds inwards; if it is too tight they will be reluctant to land. The decoys should be set so that the decoys are facing into the wind. However, do not make them too regimental in appearance. Pigeons feed into the wind as this stops their feathers ruffling up. They do still move around though, and a set of decoys all facing exactly the same way looks too unnatural. Put some of the decoys at angles and step them out by a yard or two on either side.

For a basic pattern, the horseshoe is ideal. However, if the birds are extremely thick in numbers the single pattern can be adapted to a double pattern, or 'W' shaped pattern. This will allow birds to funnel into two areas, and is ideal if you are shooting with two guns to a hide. If the wind is blustery and changes direction indiscriminately, an alternative is to set your decoys in an 'L' or 'S' shaped pattern. As with the horseshoe, do not regiment the birds, and also ensure they are spaced to allow birds

The basic design for a 'horseshoe' decoy pattern.

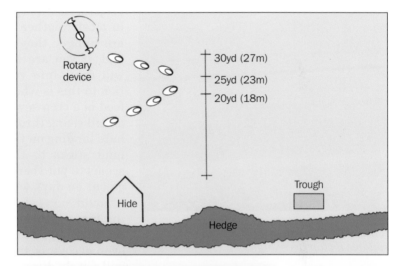

Setting the decoys in place.

A decoy set on a raised stick, which would be suitable if crops were high.

weather conditions when I suppose most sensible people would be at home, and I have found that by scattering a decoy here and there that it can draw the birds in. When the weather is bad like this, those birds that do feed out will wander about on the ground and, as a result, scattered decoys tend to pull in those that are passing over.

Having mentioned the weather, I would propose that it is possible to decoy pigeons in most weather conditions. If the birds are hungry they will travel out to feed and, if you are in the right place, they will draw into your decoys. One exception to this is when it is wet and the only food is a crop sewn on fresh drilling that is still rising through the plough. Pigeons hate landing on this sort of ground as the mud sticks to their feet, which really seems to put them off. If you do intend to go out on days when it is extremely wet, I would suggest concentrating on roosting birds rather than those feeding out. Another important aspect when shooting over decoys is that of the sun. Pigeons will not fly directly towards the sun as it has the same effect on them as it does on you when you try to shoot into it. Always try to set up so that you are not shooting into the sun and, as a result, being dazzled by it.

to land amongst them. This sort of pattern is ideal in a mixed wind, as birds will join the shape of the pattern and tend to attach to it or amongst it as and where they can.

When shooting in a mixed wind, it is difficult to judge how the birds will fly into the decoys. If the wind constantly changes its direction, the birds will do exactly the same. An 'L' or an 'S' shape pattern will allow the birds to pick their direction without forcing them to have to pull into a horseshoe or 'W' shaped pattern. If the weather is really bad and you are suffering with wind that blows from all directions of the compass, or if there is rain or drizzle, you may find it easier to set a totally random pattern. I have shot in

Roosting Decoys

If you are shooting close to trees, a great trick is to set some decoys within the tree line to attract birds into the area and among the trees as well as to the ground. Decoys that are set within the tops of trees act as confidence boosters and really help pull birds into the area. If you watch feeding pigeons you will often see the odd bird sat in trees observing the surrounding area and the feeding ground. These birds seem to act as scouts or lookouts for the rest of the flock and will be the first to become airborne at the sign of any threat. Setting a pair of decoys high in the tree line is a great addition to your decoy pattern. You can buy a set of lofting poles that extend to a range that is perfectly adequate to reach the lowest branches of a large tree at least. These poles then have a 'T' shaped attachment that is set on the top. On each end of the attachment a full-bodied decoy is placed. This gives the impression of a pair of birds sat on a branch watching the world go by. This method of decoying can also be a useful trick when roost shooting.

It can also be worth placing the odd bird amongst elder and ivy clad bushes, but only if they are going to be visible to the birds flying around the area. If you take a full-bodied decoy or a shell and place a piece of wire through the decoy, you can then use this to tie and hold it in place. Another trick is to set a couple of crow decoys along a fence line. Take a full-bodied decoy and simply use a stick to raise it off the ground and set it next to a post on the fence. This will not only draw in pigeons that will see the roosting crow as a confidence booster, it will also pull in jackdaws, rooks, crows and possibly even magpies that are in the area.

Mechanical Decoy Aids

Let us assume that you intend to use a pigeon rotary device or mechanical flappers and peckers to aid your chances of decoying in birds. It is all very well thinking that you can simply place these wherever you wish, but in reality if you do this you risk scaring off the birds rather than attracting them. Flappers and peckers can

be brought into a pigeon pattern, and a couple set up amongst the pattern and facing into the wind will be useful. It is the rotary device that you need to set in the right location. The idea is that it gives the appearance of birds flying into the decoys and it is therefore essential that it is set so that the birds are flying into the right wind direction. They must give the impression of birds that are about to settle and then turn into the wind.

There is no point setting a rotary device right in the middle of a decoy pattern. It should be set at the end of the pattern or in a location that will still allow real birds to fly amongst the pattern to land. If you set it in the centre it will block the flight of the birds and turn them away from your decoys. One workable option is to set your intended pattern and then to place your rotary on the end of it. You can then place some birds in a very scattered pattern on the other side of the rotary. In a sense you will have your true pattern and a second horseshoe, or shaped pattern, with the rotary pulling birds into both patterns. If you do this, you must ensure that the decoys on either side are within range. My personal preference would be to leave the setting of a rotary until I have seen birds come into the decoys. This gives you the opportunity to ensure that your decoys are in the right place, and to grade exactly where you need to place the rotary for best effect.

Shot birds

If all goes as planned, you will draw some pigeons in and hopefully manage to shoot some. As the shot birds mount up you may wish to consider adding some to your decoys to increase the pattern. If you have cradles, you can place these in between

A shot bird resting in a cradle.

the set decoys. When you set your decoys you will have left a gap between each one and this will give plenty of space to add more decoys. Always ensure that you leave the centre of the pattern as clear as you can to allow birds to fly inwards. As you fill a pattern, you can create another next to it so that the birds have plenty of choice over where to land. You do not need more than a dozen artificial decoys to set up a pattern to get you started. Even if you do set out twenty decoys, for example, this will still give room for some shot birds to be set out amongst them. I would start with fewer decoys, as too many will crowd out the pattern and deter birds from landing.

Flappers work to the same principle as rotary devices; if you put them in the wrong place they will have an adverse effect. You can set them in between decoys, but do not overdo things. You only need three or four at the most. Be careful not to set them so that they shroud out other decoys. Also ensure that they are set to indicate a bird

that is landing, and that the wind direction is again taken into account.

You can opt just to add shot birds to your pattern and simply set them on the ground. If you do this, a useful trick can be to carry a small pack of wooden kebab sticks. These can be inserted into the ground and then into the underside of the bird's head to hold it steadily in place. You can also place some birds with their wings slightly spread and, again, these sticks can be used to hold the wings down. It is important to ensure that any shot birds are either picked up and removed from the pattern or placed amongst it as part of the pattern. If you do not do this it will scare some birds off, especially if you are shooting over short stubble or grass. Shot birds left amongst the pattern will have feathers blowing in all directions, and those birds flying in seem to sense something is not right.

I must stress that the setting of patterns that I have described is the basic way of doing things for a normal day's pigeon shooting. I am talking about a day when you may bag thirty or so birds and enjoy some good sport. Some days will provide much more shooting and much bigger bags. Sometimes, no matter what you, do none of the rules seem to apply and the birds just seem to keep pulling in. If you get such a day then my advice is to forget the rules and go with the flow. If the pigeons keep dropping in, keep shooting and only worry about picking up when there is a lull in the action. I have enjoyed such days on a handful of occasions and they are very clearly etched on my memory. One occurred over clover and although we did not bag more than fifty, they were taken in around an hour and a half. On a couple of other occasions I have contributed to bags of over 200, but for me this is the exception rather than the rule.

One tricky issue with shot birds, especially in the warmer months, comes in ensuring the birds are stored out of the heat. Flies will quickly settle on dead birds. Within minutes they will become fly blown and then maggot invested if they are left out for even a day or two. To overcome this use a lightweight mesh bag to store shot birds in. This will keep them cool and will stop flies from getting to them. Another alternative is to use Hessian sacks or even a food chiller box. The problem with the latter is that they will only hold a few birds and are much heavier and harder to move than lightweight sacks or mesh bags.

SHOOTING FROM HIDES

The most important aspect of hide shooting is to ensure that you have a safe zone to shoot within. We have already discussed the importance of ensuring that you are aware of such things as power cables, livestock and foot and bridle-paths. You also need to consider such things as your own safety and that of those shooting with you. If you are sharing a hide, you need to ascertain just where you and your partner will shoot. Make sure this is agreed in advance and do not deviate from your agreed plan. As a rule, one of you will cover the right and one will cover the left. In this sense it is straightforward to agree that you will shoot your own side and leave the other side to your partner.

From time to time I have been in a situation when I have shared a hide with two decoy patterns. For example, a fellow shooter and I were in the centre of a large field and the birds were flying in from all angles. As a result, we set up two patterns on either side of a large shared hide. In this situation we agreed in advance to cover one side each. We then both covered a 180-degree area and ensured that we did not cross this area under any circumstances. I must admit that sharing a hide is not my favourite method of shooting. I find that if I am shooting from a hide with someone else, it must be someone I trust 100 per cent. The only other time I would share a hide is if I was teaching someone to shoot and needed to oversee what they were doing.

Sharing a hide can be an extremely dangerous thing to do and I would seriously suggest avoiding doing so unless you really have no choice. If you are in a hide with someone else, it is far safer to have one person shooting and the other observing the pigeons and marking those that fall. If you are shooting with someone else in the hide, always make sure you know where they are, and never fire at anything if they leave the hide for any reason.

If you are in a situation when you are shooting with others but from separate hides, you must ensure you know where everyone is located. Make sure that all hides are made far enough apart so that you are not in range of each other. Remember that although the killing range of a shotgun is up to 45–50yd, the shot can still do damage at up to 300yd. Air rifle pellets can also still cause damage at 100–150yd. Always ensure that if you are leaving your hide the other guns know where you are going. Do not set up in another location unless you have already agreed this location in advance. If you approach another hide make sure you announce your presence, so that the person shooting is aware that you are coming and does not take a shot.

The final comment on hide shooting safety is centred around canines. If you have a dog with you to pick up shot birds, you need to make sure you always know where it is. This may sound like common sense, but a dog that is wondering around a small cramped hide can quickly become a hazard. Your dog should be sitting in a location that does not inhibit your shooting, and that is also safe for the dog. When you are sitting in a hide you will generally hold your gun in one of three ways. If the shooting is slow it may be broken. If the shooting is really good you may have the gun loaded and cocked ready to fire. In this case it is usual to have the barrels pointing skywards or to the ground. If you have a dog I would recommend that the gun is facing skywards and not towards the ground. There is always a danger no matter how safe and careful you are that a gun could be knocked or fired accidentally. If the gun is facing the ground you will hold it at an angle away from your feet and legs. The problem is that the dog

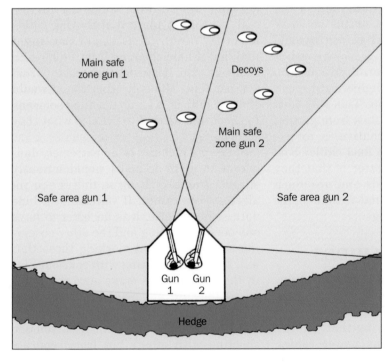

The safe arc of fire for two guns sharing a hide.

could be in the line of fire even when the gun is pointed downwards. I am not saying this is likely to happen, but it is a genuine issue that can occur and something, due to my own personal experience, that I have always been very cautious about.

Shotguns or Air Rifles

The technique of shooting over decoys will be the same no matter what gun you intend to use. You will need a hide and you will need a decoy pattern. The type of gun you use, whether a shotgun or an air rifle, is very much one of personal choice combined with situation. I feel it is fair to state from a purely pest control perspective that the shotgun is the ideal tool for shooting over decoys. You can shoot birds that are sitting or in flight. A shotgun can be chambered to hold up to three cartridges (one in the chamber and two in the breech) without needing to be classed as a firearm. If a shotgun can hold more than three cartridges, it is classed as a firearm and a firearm certificate will be needed to posses it. The noise of a shotgun will scare wood pigeons that are within the pattern or about to land as you shoot. That said, if the birds are intent on flying into your pattern they will, and it never ceases to surprise me just how many birds fly in even seconds after a shot.

The big drawback when using a shotgun is that the noise will signal your presence to anyone and everyone in the vicinity. There is nothing more annoying than trying to concentrate on your shooting only to be interrupted every few minutes by walkers who have heard the shot and decide they need to investigate further. Most walkers and other countryside users are sensible people and will accept your right to be doing whatever it is that

you are doing. Alas, some people just feel that they are duty-bound to take a closer look. On several occasions I have had people travel some distance from a footpath to see what I am doing. This is not only dangerous for them but also for you, as you have no idea what their intentions are. The other problem with a shotgun is the risk to your hearing. I have shot all of my life and never used hearing protection. Now, at 31 years old, I am half deaf and much of this is the result of shotgun shooting without ear defenders. My advice is to shoot with ear defenders and protect your hearing. After all, you cannot replace it.

The air rifle is a totally different creature to the shotgun. Although many airguns work on a bolt action system, your basic spring rifle will be single shot and needs cocking after each shot. This can become rather tedious if you only have a spring rifle or a single shot model. Additionally, you will only be able to shoot birds that have landed within the pattern, as trying to shoot a flying wood pigeon accurately with an air rifle is simply not a sensible task. There is nothing wrong with shooting pigeons over decoys with an air rifle, but do not expect to shoot huge bags. Personally, I find an air rifle the ideal tool for decoying in those areas where, as described, a shotgun would attract too much attention. I often use my air rifle when I am shooting close to areas that the public tend to frequent. I can conceal myself and carry on with my shooting without anyone noticing.

PACKING UP

At the end of your day you will need to pack up all your equipment and ensure that you have left everything as you found it. Make sure that all of the decoys are

DECOYING – 'THE EXPERIENCE'

You have spent the last week patiently waiting for the pigeons to settle on the field of barley. They have been feeding on the flattened areas of crop and you have, with the landowner's permission, set some deterrents on the surrounding crops. By watching the birds, you have established that they are flying into the crop from the far left of the field via three separate flight lines. There is a flight line also coming directly across the field but this if no way near as busy as the three coming from the left. As it is late summer, the morning is spent away from the area. At just before noon you make your way to the barley field. You stop the vehicle on the track a few hundred yards away, sit back and watch. There are birds landing in twos and threes amongst the flattened crop. In total there are in the region two to three hundred grey specs visible amongst the field of yellow stems.

A week before, the weather had been warm but the rain had pelted down. The birds were in the area but it was only when the rain flattened the barley that they finally began to feed amongst it. It was tempting to shoot the area the day after the rains as the birds were in abundance. The problem, as you had learnt previously, was that the birds would refrain from landing as the standing crops were too heavy and wet in the surrounding area. It therefore made much more sense to wait for a day or two.

After ten minutes you have established that all looks positive, the birds are still mainly flying in from the left and, as the wind is still, they are circling once before settling down to feed. Now is the time to take the equipment from the vehicle and set yourself up for the afternoon's shooting. As you amble down the track to the area the birds are feeding on, you can hear and see them as they clatter away. Within seconds all of the birds have lifted, there is no need to be concerned as they will be back.

The flattened barley is about 50yd out from the side of the hedge so you will need to try and draw the birds closer to you if you stand any chance of shooting them. You cannot set a hide up in the standing crop as this will damage it, so the wisest approach is to set the nets against the hedgerow. The hide poles are pushed into the rock-hard ground and given a tap with a mallet. The net is attached to them and a tent peg is placed on each side to hold the net a little more securely. The hedge stands some 6 or 7ft high and this gives you shelter from above so no top or roof net is required. That said, the sun is now getting rather hot so to shade yourself you place a small piece of net across the top of the hedge and half over the sides of the hides to give some welcome shade.

You then place all of your equipment into the hide and set your seat up to make sure you have a good comfortable area to shoot from and, of course, a clear line of sight to shoot in. Your cartridge bag is then placed to one side for easy access and the essentials, such as food and drink, to the other side. The next step is to set up the decoys. You take half a dozen shell decoys out into the laid crop. These are set in a loose scattered formation so that they give the impression of birds feeding on the ground. They are set to attract but most decoys will be set closer and these are the ones you will rely on to pull in the birds.

Your true pattern starts about 35yd from the hide and about 15yd from the flattened crop. You take some full-bodied decoys and set them on extended pieces of dowel rod. On the top of these are fitted the saw blade springs that will give the impression of the birds gently moving if the wind does pick up. In all, you set up ten full-bodied decoys in a wide horseshoe with plenty of room for the birds to fly inwards. You have remembered that the birds will not fly into the standing crop, but the pattern will pull them in as if to land before they can see the flattened area to land in. The decoys in the flattened area are also set in such a scattered manner that they do not make anywhere near as appealing a site as your horseshoe pattern. To top it all off you place a crow decoy on top of the hedge about 50yd out to the left to act as a confidence booster.

With the preparation done the time is now right to commence the shooting. This is truly a textbook event and the birds have been flying over even while you have been setting up the decoys. It takes half an hour or so for the birds to really gain confidence, and you resist a few long shots before finally having a crack at a pigeon that comes from the left and heads straight for the centre of the horseshoe. The bird sails in and its wings drop back ready for a landing. The bird then twists slightly to turn into the flattened crop. You are on it and, in a textbook 'move, mount and shoot' manoeuvre, you fire and the bird folds flat and drops like a stone. Over the next two hours the birds come in steadily but not too fast. Your shot to kill ratio is looking good and you have about thirty birds in the bag. Any wounded ones have been picked straight away and are now in the fly proof mesh bag beside you in the hide. A few have fallen dead in the standing crop but you know where they are and will pick them later. Half a dozen early birds have already been picked and are now part of the pattern and set on flappers with their wings spread.

The birds finally ease up in the late afternoon as the heat really picks up, so you decide to call it a day. All in all things have gone well and you feel somewhat smug and rightfully proud of your shooting. Of course, things do not always go so well; as you pack up you recall shooting the same field when it was sown as rape in the winter. The birds had fed in huge flocks but one bang and they disappeared into the distance.

Then in the spring you had shot the same field when the barley was just poking through. On that occasion you had shot from a hide in the middle of the field. The decoys had been set in two split patterns and the birds had just paired up and stopped flocking. They had pulled in a treat but for some reason you could not hit a barn door on that occasion. Mind you, in retrospect the wind had been blowing on that day and those birds were really moving. That, you remind yourself, is the joy of pigeon shooting. You experience sport that is always altering with the seasons and shooting that alters depending on your mood.

The kit being collected up at the end of the day.

collected in and that you tidy up the shot birds. It pays to keep a count of the shots and birds that you manage to drop. You also need to ensure that no birds are left wounded or injured, and that every shot bird has been dispatched. You should do this as you go along but it always pays to double check, especially if any birds have fallen some distance away.

It is worth counting the shots and birds that you manage to take. There are numerous ways of doing this. One is to purchase a small metal clicker to count the shots on. These can be quite pricy and there are cheaper alternatives. One is to place your empty cartridges in piles of hits and misses. You can then match the hits to the shot birds at the end of the day (place the second

of a double shot for one kill in the miss pile to avoid confusion). Alternatively, small plastic counters that children use for learning basic maths can be purchased from stationers, and these make ideal counting aids at a cheap price.

You need to ensure that you pick up all of your rubbish and all empty cartridges. If you have made a natural hide you can leave it intact if the landowner is happy for you to use it again. If they would prefer you to dismantle the hide, tidy all the debris that has been used and place it out of the way sensibly. If you have made a hide with netting and you have used tent pegs to secure it, make sure you collect all of the pegs and also clear any debris from your netting before putting it away.

CHAPTER 5

ROOST SHOOTING

Roost shooting is, without doubt, my fa-vourite method of pigeon shooting. While decoying is practised all year round, roost shooting is very much a winter pastime. It does not allow you to take the large bags that can be obtained over decoys. It does, however, allow you the chance to experi-ence some very fast and testing shooting that would challenge even the most ex-perienced shot if the conditions are right. Shooting over decoys is testing enough, but shooting birds that are flying in to roost fast and very randomly is something else.

The basics of roost shooting are easily explained. You locate an area where there are clear signs of wood pigeons using the trees to settle in for the night. You will look for signs of droppings and feathers across the floor and amongst the trees. You then return to the area about an hour or so before dusk and position yourself in a location where you can shoot the birds as they fly into the trees to roost for the night. Those are the basics of roost shoot-ing. Of course, there is a little more to it than that.

I particularly like roost shooting because it does not involve all of the kit and ca-boodle that you need to shoot over decoys. All you need is some warm clothing that blends into your surroundings, your gun and ammunition and possibly a bag for the shot birds. You will not need to build a hide if you position yourself within the trees and keep still, as you will be hidden

naturally in the dying light. The birds will be flying into the area of their own accord in order to roost. Therefore, you do not even need decoys, although it can help to put a couple of decoys on a roosting pole if you so desire.

BLENDING IN

The most important aspect of roost shoot-ing is to find a spot to stand where you can blend into your surroundings but also shoot comfortably. You need to have room to raise your gun to shoot, but you also need to have sight of the whole area. Find an area that offers you natural shel-ter but also space to be comfortable. You could stand against a large tree so that this naturally shelters you and shadows you. Is there a useful patch of bramble

Pigeons settling to roost in a line of trees.

99

that you can slot into or behind? Maybe a hedge runs along the side of the wood that gives you an ideal spot to shelter while also looking out for birds as they fly in. There are numerous options available but the main issue will be the size of the wood in which you are shooting. If it is a large wood and the birds are roosting in the centre, or in particular areas, you will have no choice but to shelter amongst the trees. In this case, you will often not see the birds until they are flying right above you. If the wood is small, you may well be able to stand in a spot that allows you to see out of the wood, which gives you more time to prepare for your shot and mark the bird you hope to take as you watch it fly in.

WEATHER CONDITIONS

As with decoying, the weather will play a part in your success when roost shooting. If the wind is blustery and continually altering in direction, the birds will fly in from all angles. If the wind is steady and coming in one direction, the birds will fly in with the wind working in their favour. They will then often circle before roosting, which gives them the chance to pass over the area and choose where they want to land. It is not uncommon for birds to circle a few times before finally landing at roost. The sun will also be an important factor. You will be shooting at dusk and the sun will be setting slowly. It is important to try to avoid standing in a position where the sun shines into your face, as this will make shooting extremely difficult and uncomfortable.

Rain will also play a part. The birds will roost whether it is wet or dry, but if the roost area is rather open they may opt for a more covered roost if conditions are wet. In most cases this is not an issue, as roosts tend to be in sheltered areas that offer warmth and shelter already. The problem comes in situations when you are shooting woods that are large or in close proximity. On such occasions the birds may have more than one roost spot. It is in these situations that luck can play a part. However, using your field craft you should be able to observe the roosts that are active, and you will soon learn to read the ground you cover and discover which roosts are being used in which conditions.

USING A SHOTGUN

Roost shooting with a shotgun is an extremely testing method of shooting that offers a huge variety of different shots. The pigeons will fly in at a variety of speeds and angles, and often in small groups. When this happens the key is not to get flustered, simply pick a bird and commit to shooting at it. As I have mentioned, the birds will often circle before landing. It is important to remember this. If you get a group of birds that fly in quickly and take you by surprise, do not panic and snap a shot in haste. Keep still and wait, as the chances are that they will fly round and drop a few seconds later. When this happens you will be prepared and can confidently take your shot on your terms and not the birds'.

When roost shooting, you will fire several shoots in a quick period of time. The birds will continue to roost until they are moved off by the continual shooting. If the birds are flying in well, you may be lucky enough to get a shot every few minutes. Remember to mount your gun correctly and to ensure that your shot is safe before taking it. Try to take good, clear shots and not shots that force you to fire through a mass of twigs, which can deflect the shot. Also remember that you are firing up into the trees and that from time to time debris will fall down. There is nothing more painful than getting a small piece of twig or leaf in your eye. I have suffered this on many occasions and it can quickly put an end to your sport for the day. I am not suggesting that you have to wear shooting glasses (this is of course an option), I am simply saying that if you fire at a bird directly above you, turn your eyes away from the debris after the shot.

It never ceases to amaze me just how swiftly pigeons suddenly seem to appear when you are roost shooting. One minute everything is quiet and then all of a sudden you hear the clatter of wings amongst the branches above you. Next, a flash of grey appears to your front and then another to the right. The birds start to settle and, even as you fire, then another pair is already circling or preparing to land. As you shoot, remember to mark any shot birds and to note where they have fallen. It is important that when you stop for the day, you make every effort to pick up all of the shot birds and your empty cartridge cases.

USING AN AIR RIFLE

I am equally as keen on shooting roosting pigeons with an air rifle. Although the principle is the same, the big difference, as with decoying, is that you will need to shoot birds that have landed. As a result, you need to ensure that the area you choose to shoot offers you good, clear shots into the tops of the trees. As we have already discussed, branches can deflect shotgun pellets and many a pigeon has been saved by a fortuitously placed branch. If a branch is in your way, you

A single pigeon at roost. The branches will present deflection for air rifles and shotguns alike.

need to really ensure your shot is well placed when you are firing a single pellet with an air rifle.

I would suggest that you pick a spot where you can settle up comfortably and be within range of a nice, clear roost spot. If this is within a wood, you can sit quietly and wait for the birds to fly in. Before shooting, you need to assess the areas that are going to give you those all important clear shots, as opposed to those that are too sheltered. Try to resist shooting at birds that land in areas where the cover is clearly going to obstruct your shot. Use these birds as confidence boosters to draw other birds into your chosen location. Also make sure that you set up in an area where the pigeons are going to land within a sensible distance for you to achieve a 'kill' shot. There is no point finding a perfect roost and settling down, only to discover that your target is 10yd out of range.

The author roost shooting from the cover of some old logs as the birds fly into the surrounding trees to roost.

Another point to consider when roost shooting with an air rifle is the light, as it will influence your shooting. You will be shooting at dusk and the light will rapidly be falling as the birds come in to roost. If you are shooting with open sights you will find that the darker it gets, the harder it is to pick a clear point at which to aim and shoot. The same applies with a telescopic scope, especially if it is a basic one. Scopes can be purchased with no end of light saving gadgets and enhancers. These allow you to shoot further into the dusk and help to ensure a clear image. The drawback is that many of the really high quality scopes will cost as much as, if not more than, some air rifles. A good tip if you are using open sight is to place a dot of luminous paint onto the tip of the sight. This will help you focus your shoot on a set area, and makes shooting a little easier.

ORGANIZED PIGEON DAYS

Although it is now a dwindling aspect of pigeon shooting, one extremely useful method of roost shooting is to arrange a pigeon day or roost event. In the past these were incredibly popular, and would often be carried out in February for pigeon shooting and in May for corvid shooting. Unfortunately, in recent years the fact that these are extremely good methods of dealing with a pest species has been overshadowed by the sporting aspect. Those who are opposed to shooting and hunting have used the 'sporting' aspect of pigeon shooting as a tool to make such events seem and sound rather 'inhumane' and unnecessary. The image has been created of gun-toting camouflage clad hunters taking pot shots at anything and everything that moves. This is, of course, far from the reality of a genuine pigeon shoot.

The format of a pigeon day is a simple one. The whole point of pigeon shooting is to manage the numbers of the birds for pest control purposes. As we have already discussed, a lone person roost shooting will bag a few birds but will not make a huge impact on the population. Far more can be taken with the use of decoys, but this does not alter the fact that roost shooting is a viable method of pigeon control. The biggest problem is that as you shoot the birds on a roost, they will move to another roost, which may be on a neighbouring farm or on the same property but some distance away.

A pigeon day is an opportunity for neighbouring farms to co-ordinate and come together in a bid to get as many people as possible out to target the birds at one time. The idea is that guns cover as many roost spots as they can in a bid to keep the birds moving from roost to roost. In this manner, several thousand acres can be covered in one go and a great many birds can be bagged. If you have thirty guns out and they all shoot twenty birds each, this is a considerable number of pigeons in one sitting and well worth the effort. Pigeon days do not have to be limited to roost shooting alone, and it is perfectly feasible to have a stint on any feeding birds over decoys beforehand.

In recent years I have had the pleasure of partaking in several organized pigeon days and these have taken a range of formats. Every December I enjoy a morning's game shooting followed by lunch. We then set off *en masse* to cover the numerous roosts on the farm, and settle back well before dusk to make ready for the pigeons. As the birds start to fly in, you suddenly realize that the farm on the opposite side of the river is also shooting the roosts. When you fire your first shot you see a pair of birds head across the valley to the roost in the big wood that is just over the boundary. Suddenly, you hear another shot from the wood. It is a somewhat surreal feeling to realize that you are not the only person shooting, and as you pack up and head back to the car there is always a feeling of anticipation when discovering how many birds have been taken.

I have also had similar days, mainly organized to take place in February, over fresh sewn crops, and I have seen guns shooting nearly all day over decoys. I can recall one such day some ten years ago when nearly every gamekeeper and helper who had a gun set forth on a very bright but cold February afternoon. Nearly every crop at risk covering several thousand acres was covered and the birds were kept well on the move. They did not have the luxury of being able to settle, and a vast number were taken.

Corvid shooting in this manner, particularly for rooks, is something that occurs in May. This is when the young rooks are finding their wings and can be seen jumping from branch to branch amongst the light green tree canopies. The magpies and crows will also be on the move, as will the jackdaws, and these can also be picked up. In April and May many of the song birds and game birds are busy laying eggs and trying to produce young. Corvids can cause immense damage by eating eggs and even taking young chicks, so this is an ideal time to thin out their numbers.

Aside from shooting methods, corvids can also be caught in a range of traps. The Larsen trap and Rook Funnel traps are incredibly effective, as any gamekeeper will testify. Larsen traps are operated by the

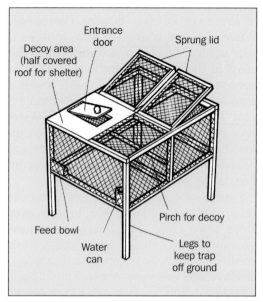

A Larsen trap.

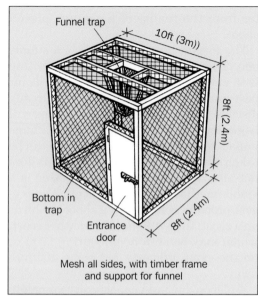

A funnel trap.

Roost shooting from a naturally formed hide in winter.

use of two sprung doors that are set either on the side or the top of two trap compartments. Opposite these compartments is a separate decoy compartment. In this compartment either an artificial or real crow or magpie is kept. The decoy bird must have food and water and the trap must be checked at least once, but preferably twice a day. The idea is that the decoy draws in other birds and they enter the neighbouring compartments which normally hold some eggs or a rabbit as bait. The bird entering the compartment will spring it shut and it is trapped until it is removed.

The funnel trap is a much larger affair and is designed to catch multiple amounts of rooks and other corvids. The trap consists of a wooden frame with mesh sides, bottom and roof. In the roof will be a funnel that is wide at the top and narrows at the bottom. The funnel will protrude into the trap for about 1½ft. Birds will enter the funnel to reach the bait or other birds.

ROOST SHOOTING – 'THE EXPERIENCE'

A cold December day sees you setting out about an hour before dusk, armed with you gun and the dog. The pigeons have been hitting the surrounding fields of turnips and rape. The problem is that, as they are flocked, they are really hard to decoy. You have seen the birds passing to and from and they have numerous flight lines passing across various locations. The main body of pigeons are roosting in a large wood some 30 acres in size. This is an ideal location in which to shoot them, but you need more than one gun to cover the wood. If you try and shoot it alone the birds will just move further along the wood and your attempts will be futile.

You have therefore opted to stand under the cover of a large ivy clad oak tree that sits in a spinny that is about 400yd from the wood. A good few birds settle in and around this tree and they also pass over the spinny on their way to the large wood. You have no decoys and are trusting your instincts to be in the right place at the right time. As you settle up besides the tree, you pull your hat tight and your scarf up to cover your face from the elements and also from the birds. It is then a waiting game as you prepare for the birds to come in for the night.

The first shot takes you by surprise, a pigeon comes fast from behind you and you shoot as it is heading away from you. The first shot misses and so does the second. As you reload, another comes from the same direction. This time you are ready and, as it passes over, you are already on it. You raise the gun and the bird is fired at while it is directly overhead. The bird crashes down into the surrounding cover and the dog is sent to retrieve it. The next ten minutes sees a group of twenty or so birds fly straight into the tree you are stood by. You fluster as to which one to shoot at and rush a shot at a sitting bird that is in the tree. You miss point blank but your second shot drops another bird that has flown in just behind it.

Darkness is rapidly setting in, but the birds continue to come in and get faster and faster as the wind picks up. You have taken shot after shot in a short period of time and, as always with roost shooting, the cartridge to kill ratio is rather high. Finally, with eight birds down the pigeons seem to stop. It is now nearly dark and the time has come to head back to the yard. As always, you hang on for another quarter of an hour as you know that the 'black stuff' (rooks, jackdaws, crows and magpies) always roost after the pigeons. This pays off and you account for a very high rook and a brace of jackdaws that are heading for the hollow of an old elm tree. The day is now truly over and dusk has turned to night with the winter weather biting hard against you and the sodden dog at your heels. This is one of those occasions when a hot flask of coffee and a warm car heater are very much appreciated.

They are then unable to exit as the funnel is too narrow at the bottom.

The main idea of an organized corvid shoot is to slim down the numbers as quick as possible. The best way to do this, especially with rooks, is to stand below their roosts in the late evening towards dusk.

Rookeries can be incredibly noisy places that will spread for several hundred yards. At times there will be hundreds of rooks living amongst a rookery. The idea is that guns spread out below the rookeries and reduce the numbers by shooting the young birds as they hop from branch to branch. In addition to this, the adult birds can be taken as they fly in for the night. The secret with rook shooting in this manner is to remember that rooks can do good as well as bad. They do eat crops and they also take eggs, but this is counteracted to a degree by the amount of slugs and beetles that they consume. As a result, the aim is not to completely destroy a rookery by killing every rook, but to reduce the numbers and keep them steady. Those who understand the countryside will recognize this as a form of conservation. Not only that, but rooks make good eating and a harvest of them can make a welcome addition to your freezer.

Crows and magpies are far harder to bag by roost shooting, as they tend to live in pairs and small family groups. The secret with these is to shoot them as they fly into roost or over the trees to settle. Remember with rooks and crows that they will fly in later than pigeons so you will need to hold on a little longer than you would with the pigeons. Jackdaws will also make for good shooting but be aware they are rather tricky to shoot at roost. They often live amongst holes in trees and disappear before you can fire a shot. I often find that for crows, magpies and jackdaws a quiet

A rookery showing the nests and birds as they settle to roost.

hour or two stood in their roost area with an air rifle can pay dividends. Of course, there is no reason why you cannot arrange a corvid or pigeon day with air rifles and shotguns combined. Although, with an air rifle you will not have the added bonus of the bang keeping the birds moving.

CHAPTER 6

BARN SHOOTING

MOTIVATIONS FOR BARN SHOOTING

One type of pigeon shooting that is often overlooked is that of shooting pigeons around farm buildings and yards. This is very different to decoying wood pigeon and even roost shooting, as this sort of pigeon shooting centres mainly around the control of feral pigeons and collared doves. These two species will often take up home in and around barns, grain stores and farm outbuildings. On first impression this may seem quite acceptable, but when you take a closer look you can see why control is necessary. Pigeons living in grain stores cause an obvious problem by eating and defecating on the grain. A similar problem occurs when the birds are roosting in and around areas where straw and hay is stored. Of course, if you have storage areas where produce such as vegetables are placed prior to haulage or processing, the last thing you want is pigeon waste falling on them.

In such situations, it will be necessary to control the birds and to limit their numbers. This sort of pigeon shooting also differs from the other types discussed, as the air rifle will be the ideal tool for the job and the shotgun will only play a minor role, if any. This form of pigeon shooting is often considered as nothing more than a pest control exercise. In actual fact, it can also provide some excellent sport. It is also a brilliant way of teaching novices about gun safety and respecting their quarry, along with quarry identification.

BARN SHOOTING TECHNIQUES

Feral pigeons, just like wood pigeons, will go out to feed during the daytime. As a result, you tend to find that there are three times best suited to shooting them around buildings. Dawn, before they go out to feed, and dusk, as they return from feeding, are the ideal times. In addition to this, they will often return to sit during the heat of the day as they digest their morning feed and rest before going out to feed in the afternoon. There are also two main methods of shooting them. The first is from within a building as they sit and roost on the rafters or amongst beams and ledges. The second is to shoot them as they rest on the roof tops on the outer side of the buildings.

Safety

As you are shooting around buildings you must consider safety to be the first and foremost priority. Make sure that you are fully aware of what areas you

A feral pigeon settled amongst the rafters of a barn.

Shooting Inside

The first aspect we shall look at is that of shooting inside a building. Before you even commence any culling, you need to visit the area and carry out some basic checks. Firstly, find what area the birds tend to roost within and check for all the nooks and crannies in which they will reside. Secondly, as mentioned, check for any hazards and ensure that you avoid these. Finally, look around the building and find some spots where you can shoot from while avoiding the hazards.

With regards to the actual shooting, it is feasible to stand without any cover and simply to shoot the birds as they sit above you. The drawback with this is that after you have shot for perhaps two sessions the birds will very quickly cotton on and clatter off as you approach. The best approach is to set up by some cover such as old pallets or bales, and to use these to shelter yourself. If you set such a hide up within the corner of a barn, you will hopefully be able to leave it for some time. The hide will swiftly become part of the pigeons' surroundings and all you will have to do is to sneak in before they settle to roost.

The first thing to do before you shoot is to ensure that you have a good idea of the range at which you are shooting. Shooting indoors is something that I have always found different to shooting outside. Everything seems to be more compact and closer than it really is. I find that the best thing to do is to measure out the distance along the walls roughly from beam to beam. Beams tend to be well spaced and, as the birds will more than often sit and rest on these, it makes sense to mark your distances out in this manner. It is also important to remember that you will be shooting upwards and, therefore,

can and cannot shoot around. If you are shooting outside, ensure that you know where any power lines and telephone cables are situated. Never shoot at a bird that is sitting on the aforementioned cables, and never fire a shot that could damage them. In buildings, ensure that you know of any hazards such as lights, cables and water tanks. Again, never fire towards or at these as the last thing you want is damage caused to the property you are shooting around. You must also consider the roofing area you are shooting towards and try to ensure that no damage is caused to slates. This is a reason why the air rifle is the ideal tool. I have shot pigeons in and around buildings for years and using an airgun of up to 12lb ft has never caused any damage to the roof of a building. Another important factor, especially in old barns, is to watch out for asbestos panels and roof sheets. Asbestos is dangerous to health, so you must avoid inhaling dust from punctured sheets.

you need to compensate for this with your shot. If you do not, what seems to be a rather easy shot will become frustrating and unexpectedly difficult.

When you do start to shoot the birds, the biggest difference from decoying pigeons is that you do not need to pick the birds up as you shoot them. You stand far more chance of bagging the birds if you leave them until after you have finished shooting, as the birds will continue to be oblivious to your presence. I would suggest that any wounded birds are swiftly dispatched with another shot. Shooting internally in this way is a relatively quick process. You will often find that you are shot out within an hour or two. It is very much a pest control exercise, but to the keen airgun shot (myself included) it does also provide some welcome sport.

There are times when shooting internally from a hide is not possible or practical. You may have to shoot inside several buildings and, as a result, will be constantly on the move. I am sure you know the situation, there is the barn then the tractor shed, and adjoining this are two or three outbuildings and a cow shed. The pigeons will be roosting in all of the buildings and as you shoot in one, the birds will clatter out into another. In this case, the only way to bag birds is to use the shadows and your skill to pursue them. It may seem all too easy to shut a barn door in order to stop the birds from leaving. The problem is that this will cut out any natural light. It is illegal to shoot pigeons with an artificial light so, technically, if you did this and then turned on the electrics you could be in breach of the law. Another situation when it pays to be on the move is when you are shooting around grain

Shooting from a bale hide built in a barn doorway.

stores. These will often have high plat-
forms and walkways. These make ideal
vantage points and enable you to take
shots that are near enough level with the
birds' roosts. This is great as long as you
do not mind heights!

Shooting Outside

Shooting birds outside of buildings is a
totally different process and one that can
provide some interesting sport for both
the shotgun and air rifle shooter. There is
no doubt that using an air rifle is still the
ideal approach. The birds will often feed
around buildings in the day time. They
will also roost and sit on the tops of the
buildings. You can use the natural shelter of a farmyard to conceal yourself. Old
tyres or the shelter of a tree will be ideal
places to sit and pick your targets. You

*Shooting feral pigeons between the outside and
inside of some storage barns.*

could also use some screen netting to set
up a hide, or even a couple of hides that
you can move between. Using an air rifle to take birds from the roof tops in this
manner is an ideal process to put into play
during the day. If you really need to control the birds, you could finish up with a
session as they come in to roost.

The shotgun comes into play when
shooting in this manner, as you can potentially take birds as they fly out from their
roosts to feed, and fly back again. I would,
however, stress that you must check
whether or not it is ok to use a shotgun
for this kind of shooting. It is not just the
risk of the hazards around the yard when
you shoot. There is also a risk of a shot
bird that has been taken in flight crashing
through a window of a building or a vehicle, especially if the farmhouse is in the
same location. You will also need to consider the noise that will be made from the
echo of a shotgun fired around buildings.
With all of this considered, I would suggest that the ideal shotgun for this style
of shooting is either the .410 or a silenced
shotgun in a large calibre.

Although I suspect that some may view
this form of pigeon shooting as somewhat
mundane, it does have many advantages.
It is a great way to get your 'foot in the
door' and can often lead to some decoying or other shooting. It is also an ideal
and quick way to add some quality meat
to the freezer with little effort. Feral pigeons taste just as good as wood pigeons
and, in many cases, are so well fed that
they are fat, juicy and ideal for roasting.
This style of shooting is also an ideal way
to introduce newcomers to the sport, especially with regard to air gunning. You
will almost be guaranteed success and it
is an ideal way to teach gun safety and
accuracy in a comfortable environment.

CHAPTER 7

ROUGH SHOOTING

It is important to spend some time looking at the process of shooting pigeons, with or without other game, by rough shooting. Rough shooting is my favourite type of sport and it is the way that I learnt to shoot. It is, to me, the ideal way to get exercise and to enjoy the countryside without any pressure or stress. It is not a way to pick up hundreds of birds but that can be part of the appeal; you travel light and focus on the shooting of pigeons. Of course, you can shoot anything else that is in season, providing the landowner has authorized you to do so.

As pigeons and corvids are classed as pests, you are entitled to shoot them all year round. You can also shoot a variety of vermin at any time of the year. Aside from those species that we have already looked at, you can also shoot rabbits, rats, grey squirrels and foxes all year round. Stoats, weasels and mink can also be legally culled throughout the year. Although all of these species will play a part in rough shooting, it is the pigeon, and to a degree corvids, that we shall concentrate on. In any event, you should be careful only to shoot the species of game or vermin that the landowner has permitted you to shoot.

USING AN AIR RIFLE

Rough shooting with an air rifle is a varied and challenging sport that has gained in popularity over the past decade. All you need to rough shoot successfully, in addition to a rifle, is a good knowledge of your ground, field craft, sensible clothing, a knife and a bag in which to carry the catch. The joy of rough shooting pigeons is that it is something that can be practised at any time of the year. Unlike decoying, you do not have to sit and wait (although you can if you choose to). In the same context, you do not have to go out at dusk or dawn to catch birds flying in or out. You can go whenever you choose. The idea is to use your skill to find and locate your quarry and to take what you can when the opportunity presents itself. You will need all of the knowledge gained from decoying and roost shooting to do this, as it will help to know the pigeons' favourite roosts and flight lines. You can also plan your activity around such things as the location of water troughs, trees rich in berries and those coverts that always hide a bird or two.

The main factor with rough shooting or stalking with an air rifle is that, as we have already discovered, you will be shooting stationary birds only. As a result, you will need to plan your approach so that you are able to get in a comfortable position to shoot without scaring the birds away. There is no doubt that camouflage or green and brown coloured clothing will help you to do this, but it is not essential. It is just as important to keep warm and

Ambushing birds from the cover of some fruit storage boxes that border a vineyard.

dry in order to aid your comfort when shooting. Just try to leave the bright yellows and reds at home.

Conditions

The joy of this sort of shooting is that the location of the birds will change depending on the weather and time of year. On a blustery day, when the rain is clattering down, you will find them perched amongst the cover of an ivy bush or perhaps amongst the firs. On a bright sunny day they will be sitting on the branches of a hollow half-dead oak tree or swaying gently in the tops of the ash and willows. Then there will be the different areas that they will be feeding in at different times of the year. You can use your knowledge, just as with decoying, to locate the pigeons as you walk round. One useful tip with standing crops is to check the tram lines carefully. All too often you will find the odd bird sitting down out of sight and

you may, if you are lucky, manage to add a few to your bag.

To me, rough shooting with an air rifle is all about keeping on the move, travelling light and coming across your quarry. You can, however, take a slightly more structured approach if you so choose. You could sit tight in an area where you know the birds will pass and simply wait for them to come to you. You may choose to sit with your back against an old tree trunk that shelters you. This may give you enough cover without a hide to reach the birds that roost in the surrounding trees. Perhaps you may settle in the hedge that is a few yards from the water trough and, from there, ambush the birds as they stop for a drink. The joy of rough shooting is that it is a pastime that you can do on the spur of the moment and without a lot of preparation. Do what you feel comfortable with and do not be afraid to vary you plans or to try something different from time to time.

ROUGH SHOOTING – 'THE EXPERIENCE'

My own approach when rough shooting with an air rifle is to pre-plan an approximate route. The route will cover a range of different areas and will allow me as many chances to bag pigeons, and any other quarry, as possible. I may start in the yard and before going any further will creep into the large tractor barn. Here, there will be a pair of collared doves sat roosting in the beam joint at the far end. I stick close to the barn wall and the John Deere covers my shadow as I slowly raise the rifle and gently squeeze the trigger. The pellet connects and the second dove clatters across to the next beam. This falls to the next shot and the birds are put in the bag.

I then walk around the back of the barn and follow the track along the side of the thick blackthorn and hazel hedge. There are pigeons here but the hedge is only a few feet high so shooting is impractical. Besides, they see me well before I see them. I walk as softly as I can along the squelching mud of the Land Rover ruts and I can see the oak and ash trees in the old pit at the tracks end. Sitting amongst them are half a dozen wood pigeons blowing gently with the branches as they sway. I slow down my pace and lower my frame so that I am walking hunched with the hedge sheltering me. I turn the corner of the track and the trees are now in front of me. The track splits and I now have a hedge on both sides. I drop to my knees and crawl the few yards to a fence post and the cover of an old tree trunk. From here I just about have

a pigeon in range. It is sitting with its back to me but through the sights I can get a clear shot between the wings and the head. This will deliver a kill shot and should drop the bird stone dead. I raise the rifle and steady my breathing. I release the shot but forget to allow for the elevation and the angle and the pellet falls short and drops into the branch below the bird. This sends it and the others clattering off and me cursing myself.

My trip continues past the pit and the trees and along a downland bank. It is scattered with patches of hawthorn and blackthorn and dotted with scrub. I walk from patch to patch listening and looking for a flash of grey or a 'coo' coming from one of the clumps. To my right, I get a glimpse of grey and hear a noise coming from a bush. There sitting just 30yd away are a brace of birds busy picking at red berries. This time I cannot raise the gun without scaring them so, slowly, I lie flat on the ground. I can then bring the gun gently into place and prepare for my shot. I have a clear view all around and can see there is nothing behind the bush so I aim at the first bird. It is sideways on and the sights are set just to the side of the wing and neck. The pellet hits home and it falls to the floor flapping. The second pigeon is a little slow off the mark and I get a shot at it. I rush the shot and miss, and it flies off to safety without out a mark on it. This is a typical example of how my rough shooting trips with an air rifle unfold.

USING A SHOTGUN

Rough shooting with a shotgun is a completely different experience to rough shooting with an air rifle. You have the advantage of being able to shoot both stationary and mobile birds, and this can add some good variation to your sport. The principle is the same and you need the same skills and knowledge as with air rifle shooting. The difference comes in that you do not need to spend so much time stalking your quarry for that one precision shot. You have the luxury of that pattern of shot and, as a result, once you get within range all you need is the ability to pick your target, assess the shot is safe and then squeeze the trigger.

Air rifle shooting is very much a pastime, especially when rough shooting, which is best practiced alone. The more people, the more noise there is and the less chance you have of successfully stalking your quarry. Rough shooting with shotguns is a different process in that you can successfully practise it in company. In fact, more often than not this proves more successful than going out alone. As an example, imagine the birds are tucked up in a thick hedge line. You can walk this in a pair so that any birds that fly out can be picked off regardless of the direction in which they fly. Alternatively, you may find that the pigeons can be kept moving around if two or three of you walk an area at the same time.

Another advantage of using a shotgun is that, for those who are interested, it allows the opportunity to use working dogs. A good dog will be a great asset to the rough shooter. It will flush birds from cover and can also retrieve any that are shot. This is particularly helpful when the birds fall into those quick biting nettles, into a dense bramble thicket or into a pond or stream.

Overhead Shooting

A form of rough shooting that is rising in popularity involves positioning yourself under a flight line and taking the birds as they fly overhead. This is an extremely exhilarating form of shooting. It is like a cross between decoying and roost shooting. If you get the right location, you will have a constant stream of birds passing overhead. These will not be dropping low as they would if you had decoys out, or settling into land as if you were roost shooting. They will be passing fast and high and will present some very testing targets.

I first came across this form of shooting by accident some twelve years ago. I was shooting on a farm with my .410 and concentrating on the rabbits. I had also bagged a couple of cock pheasants and had stopped for a minute before taking the steep walk back towards my car. It was while I was stood in the fading light that I noticed pigeon after pigeon flying over a piece of ride a few yards up from where I was. The pigeons were flying straight over to take their roosts in a large wood situated some 200yd over the boundary. I stood on the ride with some tall fir trees sheltering me and bagged twenty-seven pigeons in around forty minutes. It was one of the best pigeon experiences that I've had. I have shot that ground since and never managed to repeat the experience again.

It has been something that I have achieved elsewhere, and another location that springs to mind was in an area of large mixed woodland that I used to shoot. It covered 300 acres and contained a few small ponds as well as clearings and rides. In one spot there was a lovely hazel coppice and if you stood amongst it the birds would fly continually over head. I spent many hours stood in that coppice taking half a dozen birds here and there. On one occasion, my five year old son and I took refuge in the area as a heavy rain storm blew over. While we sheltered the birds kept passing over and, despite the torrential rain, I managed some lovely left and rights at really fast moving birds.

The end result from an afternoon's rough shooting.

CORVIDS

Although perhaps not strictly rough shooting, I feel that it is necessary to talk about corvid shooting. The same rules as with air rifle or shotgun shooting apply to corvids as they did to pigeons, so we shall not go back over this. Here, I am concerned with the occasions when it may be sensible to use a live-fire rifle to control such things as magpies, rooks, crows and jackdaws. As discussed earlier, I would never use a live-fire rifle to shoot at anything that was not sat on the ground. The rule with a rifle is that if you can see any sky in the background when you mount to fire then the shot is not safe. Therefore, it is

logical to assume that shooting in the air is out of the question.

The joy with corvids is that they are often found on the ground but usually well out of range of a shotgun or air rifle. All too often you will see rooks and crows sat 100yd away. As you edge closer and closer they hold still and then, just when you are about to get into range, they gently rise and move 100yd further away. The .22 rimfire is an ideal tool to knock off these 'blackbirds' at anything between 60–80yd. The drawback is that the .22 does have a reputation for ricochets. The bullet only needs to hit a stone or a lump of mud and that tell-tale 'twang' can be heard as the bullet heads off course. As many of your targets will be sat on plough or rock hard ground shrouded in stubble, this can be a slight concern. An option that many rifle shooters have now taken to control rabbits and other small vermin is to use the .17 rimfire. This calibre fires a slightly different round, which will disintegrate when it hits its target. This includes stones and clumps of mud. The .17 is also accurate to a slightly longer range than the .22. It can easily connect with a target at 100–120yd and, although you could do this with a .22, the .17 manages the task with a little more ease. The drawback is that .17 bullets cost a great deal more than .22 rounds.

When it comes to controlling corvids the combination of a live-fire rifle and a 4×4 is the ultimate duo. You can park up at a nice distance, sit back and take a good rest to shoot from and then get to work before the birds understand what is happening. Naturally, they do eventually begin to realize, but in just a few trips you can manage to make a good impact on the species without any noise or fuss. I must stress that you can do this on foot but the example I am giving is the ideal method for pest control.

One final note on controlling corvids is required with regards to the use of dogs. I would be extremely cautious of using any sort of dog to retrieve corvids of any type. A pigeon is a pretty easy retrieve for a dog. All the dog has to do is get used to the feathers, which separate from the body surprisingly easily. Pigeons may flap a little but aside from that there is no risk to any canine. Crows, rooks and even magpies and jackdaws are a different matter altogether. They will, if wounded, peck and strike out with razor sharp talons and a dog could be injured. The other problem is that a dog will soon learn to go in hard on corvids to prevent them from scratching or pecking. This can cause the dog to then become hard mouthed (a term used to describe a dog that picks up its retrieve in a very heavy way thus damaging the carcass) and can potentially jeopardize its usefulness for retrieving other quarry.

CHAPTER 8

THE BAG

It would be foolish to write a book on pigeon shooting without dedicating some time to the use of the birds that you have shot. I strongly believe that if you are going to shoot something you should learn to prepare and cook it. The preparation and cooking of pigeons is such an easy task that even the most inexperienced cook or 'plucker' could manage it.

HANGING AND PREPARING PIGEONS

The first thing to consider is dealing with a dead bird. Pigeons can be hung for different periods of time depending on how strong a flavour you want them to have. Game birds such as pheasants and partridges are normally hung for a period of between three days to a week or more. Hanging involves the dead bird being hung by the neck without the innards being removed. As the bird decays, the innards help spread flavour to the meat of the bird. It is this process that adds to the distinct flavour of game birds.

When it comes to hanging pigeons, I would not consider hanging them for any longer than a couple of days. The amount of time over which you can hang your birds will also depend on the time of year. In the winter months the cold will help preserve the carcass as it hangs. In the summer, even a few hours can be too long if the weather is particularly hot, and the carcass will become worthless. Personally, I do not like hanging pigeons for any longer than is necessary. I normally prepare them the day after shooting, as I find the birds contain plenty of flavour without any more being added.

Pigeon meat is dark in colour and the majority of the meat is found on the breasts of the bird. There is meat on the legs and also the carcass sides, but when it comes to preparation it can often be easier just to remove the breast. As a result, you have two options when preparing a pigeon for eating.

The first option is to pluck the whole bird and to prepare the whole carcass. Plucking a pigeon is a really easy task as the feathers tend to fall out as soon as you touch them. The only drawback is that they also tend to blow and stick to anything and everything in the vicinity. Once the carcass has been cleaned and all the feathers removed, the next task is to remove the legs, head and innards. The legs can be cut at the knuckle and removed. The head should be cleared back to the neck and then cut at the base of the wing arches and neck. The bird's crop can then be pulled from the neck. Alternatively, when the bird is 'drawn' the crop can be pulled out with the innards. To 'draw' a pigeon you make a small cut from the anus to the start of the breast base. You then insert two fingers inside the bird and pull the innards out.

You should take out the guts, heart and all vital organs from the carcass. Once this is done, the inside and outside of the bird should be wiped with a dry cloth. Do not use a wet cloth to do this, as if the bird is then being frozen it can become tainted from the cloth.

The second option is only to remove the breast of the bird and to disregard the rest of the carcass. This is a simple process. Gently cut the skin on the front of the breast and then pull back the skin and feathers until the breast is exposed on both sides. Then, run a sharp knife down the side of each breast from the top of the breast bone to the bottom. The breast on either side will then fold out and can be removed from the body. An alternative method to this is to cut the breast bone at the wing joints and remove both breasts and the bone in one go. You can then either remove the bone afterwards or leave the breast intact.

COOKING PIGEONS

Pigeon can be prepared in many ways and this is part of the versatility of the bird, as it can be cooked to suit anybody's taste. You could straight roast the whole carcass and serve it with crispy potatoes, or you could stuff it with sausage meat or chicken stuffing. You could stir fry it oriental style, or perhaps you would prefer to coat the breasts in bread crumbs and seasoning and have them fried with chips. I am no five star cook but here are a few recipe ideas.

Pigeons ready for preparation for the table.

Roast Pigeon

Take one bird per person and stuff them with sausage meat, onions, carrots and swede (or whatever you prefer). Coat the outer side of the bird with butter and sprinkle with mixed herbs or spoon over some honey. Place the birds in the oven and slow roast until the birds are crispy and brown in colour. About ten minutes before serving, place some bacon over the breast or the birds to add some different flavour. Serve the birds with crispy roast potatoes and cabbage.

Pigeon Casserole

Take either whole pigeons (one per person) or pigeon breasts and place in a casserole dish full of water. Add some whole small potatoes and a mix of vegetables to the dish. I would recommend cauliflower, carrots and broccoli with swede and onions as a winning combination. Add a couple vegetable stock cubes and also a chicken stock cube to the mix after the water has boiled. Leave the dish to slow cook on the hob for three to four hours, making sure it does not boil out. The dish can then be served as it is, with the stock adding to the flavour. Once the dish is finished you can return the carcass to the liquid and add some more vegetables. This can then be simmered and the carcasses removed so that the stock can be used as a soup.

Pasta and Pigeon

To serve two people, take the breasts from half a dozen pigeons and cut them into strips about ½in (1cm) thick. Mix with some bacon and mushrooms and one or two onions, and fry lightly in a pan with a spoon full of oil. Once cooked, which will take only five minutes or so, place the whole dish to one side. Cook some pasta in whatever form you choose and, once cooked, strain and add the cooked meat, mushrooms and onion to the pan. Add chopped tomatoes and chopped garlic to the mix and gently stir it in with a pint of water, but do not allow the mixture to boil or dry out. You should stir until the water thickens to a sauce. Serve with a topping of cheese.

Oriental Pigeon

Take whole pigeon breasts and shallow fry with a sprinkling of soy sauce. Once cooked, take the mix and place in a wok. Add bean sprouts, mushrooms and whatever else you fancy to the mix. Cook until crispy and serve on a bed of rice or noodles.

Game Pie

Take a pigeon breast and cook with a mix of other game. You can use whatever you choose, but pheasant, partridge, rabbit, duck and venison are the ideal mix. Add a thick mix of stock to the cooked meats. You can use the juice from cooking with a little chicken stock. Once the mix is prepared, make or set some pastry into a pie dish and empty the contents of the mix into the pastry. Put a lid on the pie and cook in the oven until the pastry is golden brown. You can then eat the pie hot or cold. An alternative to the pie is to make game pasties, or to wrap small amounts of the mix in filo pastry to make small wraps.

This is just a small taster of what you can do with pigeon, and I hope this shows that the opportunities are pretty much endless. The other advantage is that if you are only using the breasts and you have a dog or ferrets, the carcass can be used to supplement their feed, which means even less waste.

SELLING PIGEONS

If you prefer to sell your catch rather than to use it yourself, there is nothing to stop you doing this. You will need to obtain a meat hygiene certificate if you wish to sell to a game dealer or to sell your birds for anything other than 'local consumption'. Local consumption would be such things as selling birds to a local butcher or perhaps a hotel or pub, normally in the feather and unprepared. A meat hygiene certificate can be obtained by completing a one day course that covers such things as preparation of the carcass and spotting if a bird or animal is diseased when it is being prepared. It also teaches basic health and safety practices linked with preparing game. If you do decide to sell your catch do not expect to become rich on the proceeds. A pigeon will sell for between 5p and 20p depending on the time of year and which part of the country you are in. Pigeons will be sold in the feather and the buyer will normally prepare the bird once obtained. Do not forget that if you are selling pigeons, especially in large numbers, you may need to inform the Inland Revenue.

BAG SIZES

One aspect of pigeon shooting that cannot be missed is that of the number of pigeons that should be shot in a day. This subject is contentious and tends to flare up in the sporting press from time to time. The problem is not really linked to the amount of birds that are shot. It is more about the fact that, in some magazines, articles are written or features run that show 'proud' looking shooters surrounding by mountains of dead pigeons. Personally, I have no objection to such articles and features. I can see no reason why someone should be stopped from showing how well they have shot and what they have achieved. The point that I think is often forgotten is that, although the actual shooting of the birds might be considered sport, the reason they are being shot is for pest control.

Pigeon shoots have also been criticized in recent years, as some have felt that such events give the wrong impression of shooting. I cannot see why this is. What is wrong with a group of people going out to target a pest species in a bid to stop crop damage from occurring? I agree wholeheartedly with respecting your quarry and treating it humanely. I would never abuse an animal or treat it with anything other than the respect it deserves. The problem comes in trying to convince someone who does not shoot, or understand the link between shooting and conservation, of this way of looking at things.

With this considered, should you limit the amount of pigeons you shoot in a day? For as long as pigeons, in any form, are listed as a pest species and are damaging crops that are needed to sustain people and animals alike, I can see no reason to limit the amount you shoot in a day. My own approach is to shoot only what I can use or give away, and never to waste any of the catch. I do not advertise how many birds I have taken, as I have no need to do so. That said, I am certainly not ashamed when I do manage to take a large bag. This is good for me and the farmer, and proves that all of the skills I have learnt are working.

GLOSSARY

Automatic Type of shotgun that autmatically expels and replaces its cartridges.
Airgun Rifle or pistol that operates by an air charge being used to expel a pellet.
Ammunition Term used to describe whatever a gun fires (pellets, shot or bullets).
Arc of fire Term used to describe the 'safe' area within which someone can shoot.
Bag Term given to the amount of birds shot.
Barrel Part of a gun that the shot passes down before being released into the open.
Backstop The area behind the target. This should always be solid for a live-fire rifle.
Bore Refers to the calibre of a gun and the type of ammunition it can take.
Blown Term that is used to describe damage to shot game or meat when flies lay their eggs on the meat and they become maggots.
Broken/Break Term given to a folding shotgun when it is opened.
Brace Describes a pair of pigeons.
Bolt action Firing action used in rifles and shotguns. The bolt is released and this connects the firing pin with the bullet, pellet or cartridge.
Chamber The area of a gun into which the cartridge, bullet or pellet is inserted.
Cartridges The container that holds the charge, powder, wad and shot for a shotgun.
Clay pigeon Disk used as an artificial target for shotgun shooting.
Corvid Family that includes magpies, crows, jays, rooks and jackdaws.

Crop A part of the pigeon used to store food prior to digestion. Also a term used to describe most farm grown produce.
Decoy False bird that is used to attract a real bird into a feeding or roost area.
Dove Bird similar to a pigeon. Collared doves can be shot, rock and stock doves cannot.
Discharge Term used to describe a bullet, pellet or shot being released from a gun.
DPM Term used to describe camouflage pattern on British Army surplus.
Double barrel Shotgun with two barrels (side-by-side or over and under).
Feral Type of pigeon that is often seen in city centres or around farmyards.
Fibre Type of shotgun wadding that biodegrades when it leaves the cartridge.
Firing Pin Part of a gun that connects with the cartridge to ignite it.
Firearm Term used to describe a shotgun that holds over three cartridges, an airgun over 12lb ft in power, a live fire rim or a centre fire gun.
Flock A large group of birds or the term given to the soft cover that is used over some decoys.
Flight line The route taken by pigeons to fly to and from their feeding area.
Fore-end Part of a shotgun that can be removed for cleaning and support the barrels.
Grade Term used to measure the quality of army surplus clothing.
Gun slip Item used to carry a gun. Normally canvas or leather.
Gun safe Cabinet used to store shotguns, airguns and firearms.

Hide Shelter used to conceal yourself from your quarry.

Hide pole Support used to hold a mesh or netting in place to form a hide.

Kick Term given to the feeling that can occur with a shotgun or rifle when it is discharged.

Licence General licence states which avian and mammalian creatures can and cannot be shot or trapped, and whether or not they have an open season.

Live fire Term used to describe a firearm that releases a bullet rather than a pellet.

Lead shot Type of load used to make the pellets in a shotgun cartridge.

Lever action Type of gun that uses a lever to release a spent cartridge or bullet case.

Mesh Cover used to shroud a hide, normally in a custom camouflage rather than DPM.

Magazine Part of a rifle, airgun or shotgun used to hold ammunition.

Magnet (pigeon) Type of mechanical decoy aid.

Master eye The eye you use to look down a shotgun and to sight your quarry.

Netting Cover used to shroud a hide, normally in DPM camouflage.

Over and under Shotgun with two barrels, one on top of the other.

Priest Tool used to dispatch wounded game.

Pellet Form the contents to be discharged from a shotgun cartridge or a single pellet that is expelled from an airgun.

Pecker Mechanical decoy aid that simulates a pecking bird.

Pump action Shotgun or air rifle that is manually pumped to operate the shot.

Quarry Term used to describe the bird or mammal you are hunting.

Roost The area where a pigeon or bird sleeps.

Range The term used to describe the area in which a gun can effectively kill its quarry.

Racing pigeon Domestic pigeon that cannot be culled or shot.

Scope Item attached to a rifle as an open/manual device for aiming, or as a telescopic aid to enhance the view of the quarry.

Safety catch Part of a gun used to prevent the ammunition from being released.

Side-by-side Type of shotgun with barrels next to each other.

Stock The part of a gun that is held into the shoulder for firing.

Trigger Device used to release the firing mechanism in a gun.

USEFUL INFORMATION

SUPPLIERS

BDR Trading Surplus
Surplus clothing, accessories, workwear.
www.bdrtradingsurplus.com
T: 01903 239658

Surplus and Adventure
Surplus clothing and accessories.
www.surplusandadventure.com
T: 01386 793900

MFC Supplies
Surplus clothing, survival equipment, field
sports equipment.
www.mfcsupplies.com
T: 01323 846883

Deben
Fieldsports equipment, decoys, nets, etc.
www.deben.com
T: 01394 387762

Attacc
Books, decoys, nets, knives, etc.
www.attacc.com
T: 01953 454932

Arthur Carter URAD
Field sports equipment, etc.
www.arthurcarteruradshop.co.uk
T: 0845 370 3113

Pigeon Decoys
Decoys and equipment.
www.pigeon-decoys.co.uk
T: 02890 739652

ORGANIZATIONS

The National Gamekeepers' Organisation
PO Box 1071
Bishop Auckland
DL14 9YW

*The British Association for Shooting and
Conservation*
Marford Mill
Rossett
Clwyd
LL12 0HL
www.basc.org.uk
T: 01244 573 000

WEBSITES

Pigeon Watch
Online forum.
www.pigeonwatch.co.uk

Rural Sports
Information on country pursuits.
www.ruralsports.co.uk

Clay Pigeon Shooting Association
The national governing body for clay target
shooting in England.
www.cpsa.co.uk

The British Airgun Shooters' Association
Information and advice.
airgunshooting.org

UK Shooting Breaks
Sporting breaks, including pigeon shooting.
www.ukshootingbreaks.com

INDEX

air rifles 70–74, 95, 107, 109
  CO_2 74
  hand pumped 74
  pre-charged 73
  spring powered 72
airgun law 78
arable crops 12–14, 26, 83

bag size 103, 120
bags 46–47
bangers 14, 21
barn shooting 107
  inside 109
  outside 110
  safety 107
bird preparation 117–118
  cooking 118
  hanging 117
  plucking 117
  recipes 119

calibre 59
camoflauge 29, 31, 111
cartridge bag 46
cartridges 56, 57
chamber 56
choke 59–60
clothing 28–29, 32
collared doves 19, 21, 107
corvid 18, 25–27, 103–105, 115
crow 16, 18, 25, 46, 104–106

decoy 24–27, 33, 47
  bobbing decoy 45
  cradles 40, 91–92
  dead birds 33–34, 91–92
  flappers 40, 91–92
  flexicoys 36
  flock coated 33–34

full bodied 33, 91
  location 90–91
  mechanical devices 43
  other decoys 35–36
  peckers 45, 91, 92
  plastic decoys 33
  rockers 40
  roosting decoys 15
  rotary decoys 33
  rotary devices 44, 46, 91
  rubber decoys 36
  setting decoys 88–90
  shell decoys 33
  springs 42–43
decoy patterns 35, 88–91
  double patterns 89
  horseshoe pattern 88–91
  L-shaped pattern 89–90
  single pattern 89
  S-shaped pattern 89–90
dispatching 16–17,117–118
dogs 52–54, 94

feral pigeons 11, 18, 19, 27, 107, 110
firearms 58
  .17 116
  .22 115–116
  automatic 58
  live fire rifle 115–116
  semi-automatic 57–58
Firearms Act 1968 66
firearms certificate 58, 70, 79
flight lines 22–24, 83

game dispatch tool 17
general licence 13–16
gun cabinet 66
gun care 79
gun handling 64–65

gun makes 66
gun safety 63, 66–70
gun slip 46–47

hides
   location 84–87
   natural hides 37–38, 84–87
   netting and screens 25, 38–39
   pop up hides 39
   safety 93–94
   shooting from 93

insurance 81

jackdaw 16, 18, 91, 103, 106
jay 18

knifes 48–50

larsen traps 103–104

magpie 16–18, 25, 91, 103–104, 106

organized pigeon days 102–103

pattern plate 60
permission 80, 81
pigeon calls 45
pigeon clubs 81–82
priests 16

racing pigeon 19, 27
range 62
rock doves 20
rook funnel trap 103–105
rooks 16, 25–26, 46, 91, 103–106
roost shooting 99
   with a shotgun 100

with an air rifle 101–102
   weather conditions 100
roosting 20, 23–25, 27, 90–91
root crops 13
rough shooting 111
   overhead shooting 114
   weather conditions 112
   with a shotgun 113–114
   with an air rifle 111, 114

scopes 76–78, 102
seats 48–49
selling pigeons 120
shot bird storage 93
shotgun 55, 95, 107, 110
   .410 bore 59, 62, 110, 114
   20 bore 59, 60, 62
   12 bore 56, 59–62
   barrell 56
   bolt action 58
   bores 59–62
   double-barrelled 57, 59
   fore end 56
   over and under 55, 57–58
   pump action 57, 58
   safety catch 56
   shot size 60-61
   shotgun certificate 58, 66–67
   side-by-side 55–57
   single-barrelled 58–59
   stock 56
stock doves 16, 20

vehicles 51

Wildlife and Countryside Act 1981 13–16
wood pigeon 11–13, 27, 107, 110